ARCHITECTURE
CRITICISM
IDEOLOGY

PRINCETON ARCHITECTURAL PRESS

Editor
Joan Ockman
Coeditors
Deborah Berke
Mary McLeod

Editorial Board
Alan Colquhoun
Denis Hector
Beyhan Karahan
Alan Plattus
Jon Michael Schwarting
Bernard Tschumi

We would especially like to thank Kevin Lippert for his good advice and enthusiastic support, Judy McClain-Twombly for her care with production matters, and Bob Slutzky for his generous help with the design. We are also grateful to Pellegrino d'Acierno and Robin Ziek for their contributions to making this publication possible.

Published by
Princeton Architectural Press
40 Witherspoon Street
Princeton, New Jersey

Contents

*The papers presented at the symposium have been revised by the authors for the purpose of publication.

Editorial Statement

The present publication arises from a symposium held on 13 March 1982 at the Institute for Architecture and Urban Studies in New York City. The symposium was sponsored by a group of young architects and architectural critics who had been meeting for about a year to study the subject of architecture and politics. The group had been formed initially to put together a series of public discussions on contemporary issues ranging from post-modernism to philosophies of architectural education, and to sponsor a competition for the redesign of an urban space in Manhattan; these events took place in spring 1981 under the name "Revisions." As we evolved into a study group with regular meetings, our membership came to include the following individuals: Deborah Berke, Walter Chatham, Alan Colquhoun, Pe'era Goldman, Denis Hector, Christian Hubert, Michel Kagan, Beyhan Karahan, Mary McLeod, Joan Ockman, Alan Plattus, Michael Schwarting, Bernard Tschumi, Lauretta Vinciarelli.

Our study of architecture and politics led us to realize how little attention the subject was receiving in contemporary American architectural discourse. Indeed, we found ourselves in a context in which the subject was avoided, either consciously or unconsciously, by virtually all sectors of the profession — a fact which itself seemed significant. We were obliged to widen our perspective to take note of developments occurring elsewhere: in Europe, especially Italy with the "young post-Marxists" around Manfredo Tafuri; as well as in other disciplines that already had a well-established tradition of ideological criticism. Thus it is no accident that of the three speakers invited to our symposium, one is an architect practicing and teaching in Europe; another, also European and involved in teaching architecture, was trained as an aesthetic philosopher; and the third, an American, comes from the discipline of literary criticism. All three also have been engaged in responding in some way to the Tafurian position.

As in all groups such as ours, there is diversity of opinion, and the contributions in this publication reflect individual points of view, not necessarily those of the group as a whole. Nor have we attempted editorially to avoid either redundancy or a heterogeneous content in order to appear to present an entirely cohesive and thereby "operative" publication.

However, if we refuse to cast ourselves in a polemical role, we do remain collectively committed to the introjection of an ideological argument into the current architectural debate. Without it we believe that the practice and criticism of architecture are consigned to perpetuating conservative institutional interests whose underlying values and agendas exploit our very unconsciousness of them. Our inability to arrive at a prescriptive program should not be construed as an unwillingness to continue to search for one; we also believe that at certain moments even a purely negative critique can be salutary.

We hope by this publication to initiate a wide and productive debate on architecture in the context of the critique of ideology.

The Editors

Architecture and Ideology:
Proceedings of the Symposium

Introduction

Mary McLeod

In this symposium, we hope to address the general issue of architecture and ideology. By ideology we mean those ideas, values, and images by which individuals perceive their society at a given moment. Also implicit in our use of this term is the assumption that ideology is linked inevitably to productive relations and that one of its primary functions is the legitimization of existing power structures. An alternative title to this symposium might have been "Architecture and Material Criticism." In other words, our intention is to examine approaches in criticism and practice that consider architecture as a system of beliefs and values and that explore the relationship between architecture and the existing material processes of society.

We first became involved with this subject as an issue of investigation in 1981, a year before this symposium. The dilemma was postmodernism. At that time postmodernism generally was not viewed among architects as a broad critical or historical category, but rather as a polemical movement with stylistic and social implications. Specifically, this movement included those currents that endorse the use of historical styles and imagery, that emphasize the scenographic and decorative (as opposed to compositional) properties of architecture, and that reject the social objectives of the modern movement. Although many of us were also highly critical of aspects of modern architecture — especially its urbanism and naive utopianism — we felt uncomfortable with the solutions prescribed. Not only did many postmodernist designs seem formally regressive — nostalgic for a lost past — but in the United States they also appeared to relate in some fashion to the conservative turn of contemporary American politics. The flamboyant gestures geared toward a status-seeking *nouveau riche*, the imperialistic imagery of public structures, populist rhetoric that sounded more paternalistic than democratic, and finally the increasing appeal of programs such as gentlemen's clubs, luxury hotels, and private bathhouses all suggested that this new "avant-garde" had little interest in challenging existing power structures. Its rejection of the "corporate box" was not anticapitalist, but formal and vaguely humanitarian. The box itself, as Philip Johnson's AT&T testifies so well, was only to reappear in more regal guise, crown included. Perhaps most indicative of the movement's conservative political associations were the remarks of the architects themselves. For instance, in *Harvard Architectural Review* Robert Stern wrote, 'Postmodernism is not revolutionary in either the political or artistic sense; in fact, it reinforces the effect of the technocratic and bureaucratic society in which we live ... "

In the face of such assumptions and our own desires for social transformation, not preservation, we felt the need to examine more seriously the relationship between culture and material conditions — in particular, the nature of architecture as ideology. We formed a study group in the fall of 1981. Contemporary architectural history and criticism, as we discovered quickly, gave us few grounds for further exploration. A brief account of its developments will elucidate the poverty of materialist criticism in architecture.

One of the most important premises of the modern movement was the belief that architecture played a role in forming social conditions. Like the nineteenth-century English critics Augustus Welby Pugin, John Ruskin, and William Morris, the modern polemicists Le Corbusier, Walter Gropius, Bruno Taut, and Ernst May all firmly believed in the twenties that architecture could serve as an agent of social redemption. With the implementation of measures of economy, efficiency, and technical innovation, architecture could be produced cheaply, become available to all, and thus improve social conditions. As Le Corbusier declared in his famous concluding lines of *Towards a New Architecture*, "Architecture or Revolution. Revolution can be avoided." This was a period of naive belief and optimism, however — not criticism. While both the practitioners and early historians of the modern movement were eager to link form and society, neither attempted to penetrate the myths on which their messianic faith was based, or to analyze systematically the connections between design and material processes.

The first sustained critique of the modern movement, appearing in the sixties, also arose from social concerns. Jane Jacobs's bestseller *The Death and Life of Great American Cities* (1961) and the public outcry over the Pruitt-Igoe housing project, dynamited in 1972, were its most important manifestations. This criticism, however, tended to be issue-oriented, focusing on concerns such as the death of the street, the anonymity of long corridors, the criminal dangers of elevators, and the lack of controlled semiprivate space. Most commentators, whether inside or outside the profession, attributed these shortcomings to the personal insensitivity of architects and the profession's general lack of humanity. Few attempted to understand architecture as a broader system of beliefs and material processes, which exist in relation to economic and social structures at large.

By the early seventies, architectural criticism concentrated increasingly on formal issues and the question of meaning. Like the New Critics in literature, Colin Rowe and several colleagues at Cornell rigorously dissected the formal structures of designs. Charles Jencks, George Baird, Françoise Choay, and Mario Gandelsonas adapted concepts from semiology and structuralism to architectural analysis. And Christian Norberg-Schulz introduced a phenomenological perspective to design and criticism, reinforced by the popular reception given to Gaston Bachelard's *Poetics of Space*. What these widely divergent approaches shared was a synchronic viewpoint, which disregarded changes in the nature of ideology itself. The contemporaneous European typological studies also treated architecture primarily as a static artifact, despite their purported interest in history and political transformation. Architects such as Aldo Rossi, Vittorio Gregotti, and Rob Krier viewed type as a "constant" in a context of changing productive relations.

Current popular criticism, if indeed it warrants such a name, is best characterized as pluralistic, eclectic, and *ad hoc*. A reaction against both the moral determinism of functionalism and the reductive codification of structural and semiological analyses, contemporary criticism (most notably the writings of Charles Jencks, Paul Goldberger, Suzanne Stephens, and Tom Wolfe) embraces history, though any attempt to understand history as a dialectical process linked to class structures, no less the role of ideology in maintaining power relations, is rejected outright. The inclusiveness of such approaches, their generous and often indiscriminate humanism, essentially prohibits any systematic analysis of ideology. Genuine theory, "scientific knowledge" — always a difficult construct in regard to ideology — is impossible, even as a relativistic attainment, in the face of such divergent, and highly individual, concerns (and disregard of social life).

Twentieth-century architectural criticism and theory thus appeared to us as largely divorced from systematic ideological investigation. The naive utopianism of the modern movement, the social criticism of the sixties, the semiological analyses of the seventies, and contemporary eclectic approaches — all fail to examine architecture's "real connection" to material processes. Although architecture of all the arts is most directly tied to economic and social conditions given both its scale of production and public use, the field contains almost no tradition outside the Soviet Union of Marxist criticism or Marxist avant-garde practice. During the thirties, when in the United States art historians such as Meyer Schapiro and Clement Greenberg, strongly influenced by Marxist theory, sought to reveal the ideological nature of painting and sculpture, no equivalent socially based criticism emerged in architecture. Even the Frankfurt School — Theodor Adorno, Max Horkheimer, Leo Lowenthal, Walter Benjamin, and Herbert Marcuse — largely ignored architecture. There exists no Marxist study devoted to architecture comparable in scope and quality to Lukács's investigations of the novel or Adorno's analysis of music. Only recently, in Italy, can we see a historical, materialist criticism beginning to develop. Two approaches, strongly influenced by Marxist theory, can be discerned.

The first, based on the theories of Galvano Della Volpe, grants architecture an epistemological value equal, though not identical, to that of science and history. A reaction against both the sociological reductivism of much Marxist cultural theory and the idealism of traditional aesthetic theory, this position treats architectural meaning neither as mystification, a blurred image of some more valid (i.e., scientific) reality, nor as a privileged, metaphysical truth detached from instrumentality. Architecture contains a knowledge that is coherent and rational. For Della Volpe and architects, such as the GRAU group in Rome, aesthetic effect is always inseparable from conceptual meaning: image and concept are concomitants. Nevertheless, architecture, like other arts, possesses a certain degree of autonomy; it has its own code. Thus, historical and sociological bonds do not condition architecture mechanically and externally, but remain inevitably a part of any design's intellectual and structural substance. The very intelligibility of the image, whether representational or abstract, is grounded in experience and history. Although this position may appear to be a retreat from direct political engagement, it offers architecture, and culture in general (as Gramsci's theories did earlier), the possibility of generating new content. New contents demand "new and original forms." To the extent that architecture can generate such forms, it plays a positive, if limited, role in the creation of new material relations.

The second position, expressed most forcefully by Manfredo Tafuri, Massimo Cacciari, and Francesco Dal Co, establishes a more direct tie between architecture and material relations. In contrast to Della Volpe's interpretation, it views architecture as pure ideology, in which ideology is defined as "false consciousness" — that is, as a reflection of dominant class interests. Architecture thus plays a negative social role: it becomes an instrument of the existing power structure. Even purportedly critical architecture (and in this category Tafuri places all utopian impulses in architecture since the Enlightenment) contributes in its uselessness and, more seriously, in its deception to the perpetuation of bourgeois capitalism. Avant-garde practitioners, retreating into a reflected image of reality, have overestimated the power of the image to generate change. Even irony and silence — pure form — have lost their "cathartic power." For Tafuri, revolutionary architecture is impossible. The critic's task is to destroy the ineffectual myths, which so often have given architects false hopes for social transformation through design. The architect's only option is to find a course for revolutionary praxis outside the traditional boundaries of his field.

The following papers will address these emergent positions. Demetri Porphyrios's essay, following Tafuri's position, argues for a separation between criticism and practice; only the former permits an understanding of architecture's role as an ideological practice. Tomas Llorens's article, through a detailed critique of Kant's epistemology, warns against the defect of two of the most pervasive attitudes in architectural theory: positivism and structuralism; both ignore the problem of historical necessity, and hence the problem of choice in social transformation. Fredric Jameson's paper grants architecture the possibility of a positive role in the creation of a new culture, one (if only as an enclave within a larger order) that might ultimately contribute to structural change.

A synthetic position can hardly be defined from such divergent approaches. It is our hope only that these papers will help to open discussion concerning the nature of architecture as ideology. With Fredric Jameson, in *The Political Unconscious*, we wish to continue to ask:

> How is it possible for a cultural text that fulfills a demonstrably ideological function, as a hegemonic work whose formal categories as well as its content secure the legitimation of this or that form of class domination — how is it possible for such a text to embody a properly utopian impulse, or to resonate a universal value inconsistent with the narrower limits of class privilege that inform its more immediate ideological vocation?

This question, in the face of a highly conservative political and cultural climate, appears to us, as practicing architects and critics, central to our own endeavors.

Pieter Bruegel the Elder, The Tower of Babel, 1563

Introduction

Demetri Porphyrios's contribution to the Revisions symposium is the most explicitly programmatic of the three papers presented. That is to say, Porphyrios, having outlined a potentially comprehensive and rigorous definition of architecture as ideology, proceeds to focus mainly upon the specific tasks and tools of the critical historian of architecture in relation to that definition. This emphasis gives to Porphyrios's paper the character of a refreshingly direct methodological agenda. The positive precepts, and more or less concealed pitfalls, of this intellectual practice manifest themselves with a degree of confidence and authority that belies not only the extraordinarily demanding nature of the enterprise proposed (and the corresponding paucity of practical paradigms), but also the tour de force of intellectual synthesis by means of which Porphyrios has constructed his position. It may, therefore, be appropriate to call attention to certain implications and affiliations embedded in the argument.

In the course of his paper, Porphyrios calls attention to his recently published study of Alvar Aalto, *Sources of Modern Eclecticism*, presumably as an example of critical history at work. Indeed, in the Preface to that book he notes that "the methodological rules of historical research to which this book refers are still unformulated — at least in the branches of art and architectural history." Thus, one might read Porphyrios's paper as a kind of methodological prolegomenon, or afterword, to a book that claims to take "Aalto as an historical case study." In fact, the achievement of that book is intimately connected to the more general project outlined by this paper: in attempting to divest both Aalto and his work of the mythical aura cultivated by the architect and disseminated by the prevailing historiography, Porphyrios proposes to reverse the process by which "architecture as ideology naturalizes and dehistoricizes a historically created reality." Just as Aalto's work and its subsequent presentation by the historians of modernism seem to exemplify what Porphyrios has called "mythification," the prescription of critical history is in some respects symptomatic of what might be called a "postmodernist" — or more precisely, "poststructuralist" — mistrust of accounts based upon either the individuality of the creative subject or the absolute autonomy of the "life of forms." Both Vasarian biography and Wölfflinian formal analysis are equally suspect, along with their more up-to-date reincarnations. From the point of view of critical history, they are at best partial truths, which ultimately serve to conceal or propagate, rather than to expose, myth.

Thus, it may actually be easier to characterize and situate Porphyrios's position in terms of its aversions and warnings. It seems to share with contemporary Marxist thought, especially in its Althusserian version, a wariness of naive positivism and empiricism, without accepting any categorical distinction between "science" and "ideology." This unwillingness to speak in terms of scientific "truth" and ideological "error," but rather to focus upon "truth" as it must always be constructed and delimited within a particular discourse, is clearly related to the analyses of power and institutions developed by Michel Foucault, as is much of the vocabulary employed. These are demanding masters even within their own chosen fields of investigation. Taken together, and applied to the project formulated by Porphyrios, their strictures contribute to a picture of the critical historican on a tightrope: poised between the illusion of transcendental objectivity and the free-for-all of relativism, between the contamination of a partisan position and the impossibility of operating outside of all discourse, and between the specificity of architecture (and various architectures) and the generic function of architecture as ideology — as the naturalized representation of structures of power and production.

The position described is not entirely unfamiliar, and seems to pose, by means of an exceptionally rigorous and forthright exposition, one of the central problems raised by the symposium. Here and elsewhere the echoes of Manfredo Tafuri's claim, at the end of *Progetto e Utopia*, that there can be a class critique of architecture but not a class architecture, still reverberate. Both Tafuri and Porphyrios apparently would replace the revolution of the architectural avant-garde with the perpetual vigilance of the critical historian. In Porphyrios's formulation the role of the architect and the role of the critical historian of architecture are opposed quite dramatically, and perhaps irreconcilably. The former is involved, willy-nilly, in the mythification of social reality, or as Porphyrios has put it elsewhere ("Classicism Is Not a Style," *A.D.* 5–6, 1982) in more specific and positive terms, the mythification of construction. In either case, the intention, or at least the result, is an attempt to extract architecture from the contingency of mere style, and ultimately from history. But myth, however naive, is never innocent, and the critical historian has the incessant task of continually exposing myth and reinjecting it into the history it seeks to mask or escape.

The goal, and presumably the pay-off, of this critical enterprise is, according to Porphyrios, "freedom of consciousness" or a "state of understanding," which sounds somewhat

Socratic and subjective, but should probably be understood in relation to the theoretical tradition of Western Marxism from Gramsci through the Frankfurt School. The open question — and one which seems to lie outside the field of critical history per se — is whether the freedom of consciousness made available by the critical project of "demythification" includes the freedom to manipulate creatively the myths that have been themselves the agents of manipulation.

Alan J. Plattus

On Critical History

Demetri Porphyrios

Architecture as a discursive practice owes its coherency and respectability to a system of social mythification. In other words, a given architectural discourse is but a form of representation that naturalizes certain meanings and eternalizes the present state of the world in the interests of a hegemonical power. Architectural discourse, in that sense, is totally transparent to ideology. Its status as ideology derives from the fact that it reflects the manner in which the agents of an architectural culture live the relations between architecture as production and architecture as institution (institution here is defined as a system of norms or rules that is socially sanctioned). This means that, in the last instance, architectural discourse as ideology is related to the everyday experience of production systems and of institutions without being thereby reduced to a theory of subjective consciousness.

Thus architecture as ideology has a social function: to insert the agents of an architectural culture into practical and aesthetic activities that support or subvert (in varying degrees) the hegemonical power. "Power" and "hegemony" are used here in the sense proposed by N. Poulantzas: power meaning "the capacity of a social group to realize its specific objective interests"; hegemony indicating that the process of realization of interests need "not be reduced to pure domination by force or violence, but rather comprises a function of leadership and ideology by means of which social relations are founded on active consent." In that sense, architecture as ideology comprises not merely scattered elements of building knowledge and notions of design, but also the whole process of symbolization, mythical transposition, taste, style, and fashion. Reality, therefore, gives to architecture a set of rules and productive techniques while, in its turn, architecture gives back to reality an imaginary coherence that makes reality appear natural and eternal.

Critical history, therefore (as opposed to historiography, i.e. the infantile wish to "find the murderer"), is concerned with the project of constituting this imaginary coherence. In studying the way in which architecture as ideology naturalizes and dehistoricizes a historically created reality, critical history con-

16

fronts myth exactly where it is most successful. That is, precisely when "it goes without saying"; when it safeguards an established position from doubt or attack; and when it universalizes history by saying, "that is the way it must be." Critical history examines, that is, the process of naturalization of architectural ideology into myth.

Such is the task of critical history. Its aim is to constitute the discourse of the architecture under study insofar as it is structured by relations invested in institutions and historically determinate myths.

It should be stressed here that the project of constituting the discourse of the architecture under study does *not* imply the activity of a subject. Instead it designates the material existence of certain rules to which the subject is subjected once it takes part in discourse.

Now, in undertaking such a project of constitution, the critical historian will have to follow a number of steps. First, he has to describe the rules of classification, ordering, and semiosis of the architecture he studies. In other words, he has to describe the traditions and mental habits (always anonymous and historically determined) within which the architecture under study addresses a) the classification of the program and form, b) the compositional syntax of the plan, section, and elevation, and c) the techniques of symbolization. Secondly, he has to ask: what is the internal economy of such rules of classification, ordering, and semiosis, and how do they manifest themselves in the chosen rules of design? And further, what are the relative relations of subordination and hierarchy that organize such rules of design into a seemingly coherent aesthetic? Third, he has to ask: what is the instrumental significance of such rules of design; that is, why and in what semantic context are they consciously or unconsciously selected in the first place; and inversely, why and in what semantic context are they allowed to be recognized as operative truths, that is, as popular, everyday statements, enjoying a "natural" matter-of-factness.

In my book *Sources of Modern Eclecticism* I have attempted to undertake such a project within a concrete historical study of the work of Alvar Aalto. In this book, I first examine the design tools with which Aalto attempted to "transcend" the mere facticity of the building program and of industrial production itself. Initially, I describe his classificatory and ordering thinking — the particular techniques he employed in organizing both the building program and the plan, section, and sensuous iconography of his buildings. In examining the way Aalto conceives of the elements of architecture and of their rules of combination, I investigate his significatory thinking; that is, the particular techniques he employed in investing his design gestures with meaning. From such an analysis a number of design categories emerge as characteristic of Aalto's work: *heterotopia, particularization, typology,* and *metaphor.* Then I attempt to show the ideological functioning of these design categories. I ask, *why* and *in what* semantic context were they allowed to be recognized as operative truths? I examine, for example, the mythology that industrialized Europe wove around the concept of nature and the way Aalto's naturalism functioned within such an ideological *a priori.* And I examine the myth of the country-city debate and the way Aalto attempts to cushion its contradictions. But above all I examine the way in which the design categories of heterotopia, particularization, typology, and metaphor are articulated within economo-political life by the mediation of naturalized myths and institutions. In other words, I attempt to show how the myths of *Lebensphilosophie,* of agglutinative and heterotopic planning, and of quotational and historicist commentary (all of which were to lead progressively to the hegemonical ethos of modern eclecticism) were in the 1950s and 1960s calculated attempts on the part of architectural culture to regain the *aura* that modernism had eradicated from buildings. However, the particular historical argument and the structure of power relations I analyze in this book do not concern us here.

Now it seems to me that there is a political dimension to critical history: its *raison d'être* is the constitution of architecture as discourse and — in the process of such constitution — the unmasking of the process of mythification wherever and whenever it takes place. Such an understanding of historical constitution as a project of demythification, however, poses two questions. First, does critical history expose ideological error? Second, is critical history free from error so long as it refrains from the construction of an alternative point of view?

Does critical history — in demasking the process of mythification — expose ideological error? Of course not, for there is no ideological error to start with. Ideology is *not* a matter of truth or error. To apply to architectural history the opposition between ideology and science, that is, the opposition between false consciousness and objective truth, is but a futile exercise in morality.

We know — I hope — since Nietzsche that the opposition between false consciousness and objective truth is but one of those petrified examples of empiricist thought that we may stumble across but eventually remove. Architectural ideology is *not* an instance of error, but rather an instance of naturalized rhetoric. It is necessary here to grasp the concept of architectural ideology as a process of mythical structuring that aims at the reproduction of relations of power. Myth is motivated both by the desire toward naturalization (i.e., omnipotent power over normative behavior) and the desire toward ideality (i.e., constitution of a realm where consciousness can recognize itself as subject-constituting). Architectural ideology masks not because it is in error but because its role is to justify the very social reality of which it is the cement and nourishment.

Since architectural ideology, therefore, is not a matter of holding the right or the wrong view, but a matter of holding the "necessary" view, it can only be assumed that the aim of critical history is *not* to expose ideological errors. It simply describes the way by which myth assumes a natural attitude, that is, both an attitude of normative behavior and one of ideality. In other words, critical history describes the production of structures of normative behavior and of systems of subject-constituting consciousness.

The second question concerns the issue of the historical objectivity assumed by the historian — the issue of engagement, of *prise de position*. Can critical history as a project of demythification be free from error so long as it refrains from the construction of an alternative point of view? The question, thus stated, clearly implies that demythification is erroneous when it is practiced *from* a point of view, that is, *from a prise de position*.

This, in my view, touches the core of the argument. For, if critical history — here understood as an incessant project of demythification — sets out, by the very definition of its aims, to examine the process of naturalization within a socially constituted architectural language, it is necessary only that it assume a certain stance within history. In other words, critical history, in order to expose any process of naturalization (i.e., any power processes of normative behavior and of subject-constituting consciousness), must approach architectural discourse as a process of structuring between architecture as production, architecture as institution, and architecture as ideology.

This process of structuring is not and cannot be objective or benevolent, for it is a process of reproduction of the relations of power. This is why systems of architectural meaning are masked: not because they are erroneous but because their *raison d'être* is to articulate the relations of power while presenting them as a natural and matter-of-fact common sense. And inversely, any attempt to expose this process of structuring between the productive, institutional, and ideological levels of architecture is not and cannot be objective or benevolent. Critical history conducts its analysis from outside the discursive site defined by its subject matter. That is the only sense in which it can be said that critical history conducts an objective analysis: objective inasmuch as the critical historian lies outside the discourse that he analyzes. This "lying outside" the discourse means that the critical historian lies outside the practical, instrumental dimension with which the architecture he analyzes is implicated. He lies outside the notions, representations, images, modes of action, gestures, attitudes, and practical norms that govern the architecture he studies. In this sense, he stands outside its fictive "reality": for the function of this fictive "reality" is the naturalization of relations of power, and its success is the degree to which it remains unknown as fictive form.

But the project of demythification does not allow the critical historian to be objective in a transcendental sense. Objectivity here is *not* a mode of achieving absolute truth — not because absolute truth does not exist, but because absolute truth as a historical category does not refer to the objectivity of the historian as a subject but to the objective determination (i.e., objective, historical determination) of ideologies, a determination that is largely independent of individual subjects and accountable only in historically concrete analysis itself (a notion, incidentally, that predates Marx and goes back to Helvetius and even Bacon).

Having said this, however, it should not be understood that critical history is but an endless chasing of fleeting shadows. Critical history is not a theory of historical relativism. It is a project of demythification as a gnoseological tool. The gnoseological contribution of critical history, of course, is not similar to the gnoseological contribution of empirical science. The aim here is not to prove, not to explain, not to verify, not to create models that are intended to prognosticate. Instead, the aim of critical history is to make one see the petrified "idols of the market" (to use an expression of Francis Bacon). In other words, to make one see the realm of the forbidden, to see the "deafened words," the censures (but also to see utopia as a process of reification); so that one might achieve — if, alas, only momentarily — a state of freedom of consciousness (that is, a state neither of power, nor of doubt, nor of utopia; but of understanding).

And yet, since the project of demythification is always performed from a historically concrete *prise de position* (i.e., not from a subjective stance but from a historical stance), its findings cannot avoid being themselves "deafened words." That is to say, critical history itself is always implicated in another discourse from which it conducts its project of demythification.

And inversely, since the project of demythification is

20

anchored on the horizon of an assumed social naturalization of ideology, it runs the risk of being interpreted as a general theory of value-free relativism, which would eventually lead to an intellectual formalism.

Perhaps it is now clear where the danger lies in the analysis that structuralism has undertaken in the last two decades. This is not to say that structuralist thought is to be discarded, for it remains the most effective mode of analysis we possess. It only means that it should be qualified vis-à-vis not the nature and role of its technique of demythification, but rather the double illusion it nurtures: the illusion of power and of value-freedom that the project of demythification engenders. For the moment the critical historian has unveiled the process of naturalization of an architectural discourse, he might be tempted to believe he has discovered a truth that could now serve as a normative guide for future conduct. Or inversely, the awareness that the findings of critical history are themselves "deafened words" might lead one to the empty view of vulgar relativism.

How can we prevent, therefore, critical history from becoming the prisoner of this double illusion: the illusion of power and its paradoxical opposite, the illusion of value-freedom? Having traversed the trajectory of structuralism, the authentic problem we are confronted with now is how to construct a history that — having removed the ideological obstacles that conceal the power structures — can avoid the double temptation of turning either into therapy or into value-free formalism. And instead, how can it manage to act effectively on reality by forcing reality to reorganize itself?

It should be remembered here that I of course speak of reality (that is, historically concrete reality) and not of its particular individuals as constitutive subjectivities.

Critical history, therefore, should be understood neither merely as an interested and politically engaged strategy of demythification, nor merely as an exorcism of diseases, nor simply as a theory of rhetoric — the universal doubt of which incessantly recoils onto the critical historian himself.

Critical history should be understood primarily as a profound struggle toward achieving freedom of consciousness. That is, achieving a state of consciousness that affords a glimpse of the articulation between history and the subject, and of the relation between the subject and that which is not yet.

Francisco Goya, Saturn Eating His Own Children, *c. 1820—1822*

Introduction

Although the major part of Tomas Llorens's text is concerned with a detailed critique of Kant's epistemology, its underlying theme is the problem of the status of historical knowledge. Llorens's contention is that successive interpretations of Kant's philosophical systems have given rise, especially in the realm of artistic theory, to a point of view that ignores the problem of necessity.

This point of view was in part developed as a critique of positivism, according to which "positive" history was held to have naturalized historical knowledge on the analogy of the physical sciences, and to have reduced history to a succession of facts whose meaning could only be derived from uncritically accepted ideology. Llorens accepts this critique, but claims that the neo-Kantianism on which it rests — and of which structuralism was the culmination — replaced positivism by a formalism that, in its emphasis on the epistemological basis of artistic form, embarked on an equally reductive course. Art was reduced to the play of the arbitrary sign; it was disconnected from any ontological ground, and from any concept of what *ought to be the case*. This "ought" is seen by Llorens as the consciousness of necessity, by means of which culture transforms the brute necessity of nature. History is the process of this progressive transformation.

Llorens's text is, thus, an oblique criticism of two of the most persistent attitudes in the architectural discourse of the last fifty years: positivism and structuralism. The first, at the hands of the twentieth-century avant-garde and its later followers, gave up the attempt to provide history with a meaning to the extent that it reduced architecture to mere technique (in the modern sense of that word). The second retrieved the nonfunctional value of artistic representation, but in terms of a meaningless play of forms disengaged from any sense of historical purpose or ontological necessity.

Llorens's analysis of Kant, drastically simplified in the above summary, shows the extent to which we are the inheritors of the unresolved contradictions of Enlightenment thought — not least in some of the unconscious assumptions that lie beneath contemporary architectural polemics.

Alan Colquhoun

On Making History

Tomas Llorens

... how can an addition be obtained when the
first addendum disappears as soon as the second
enters into the sum? In order for a whole, or a
whole series, to be conceivable in time ... it has
to be possible, at least indirectly, to fix every
moment without thereby losing the general
character of time as transition and progress.

It is not only a question of establishing
and "apprehending" the moments of time, but of
repeating and recreating them! The "synthesis of
apprehension" has to act as well, and by the
same indivisible act of foundation as a "synthesis
of reproduction." Only thus will it be possible to
intertwine the present and the past, to conserve
the past in the present, and to conceive of them
conjointly.

Ernst Cassirer, *Kants Leben und Lehre*

When we say of events that they "make history," the
expression, compared with other similar expressions
such as "making poetry" or "making science," seems to
entail a metonymic displacement: from the activity to the object of
the activity, the latter being therefore endowed with the active
character of an agent or a subject.

The coincidence of subject and object makes history
appear to "make" itself. This naturalization recalls its origin in
the Greek term *historic*, in which it designated the profane and
impartial observation and record of events, in opposition to
mythos, the sacred and partisan narrative of the memorable origins of the community. In expressions such as "clinical history"
or "natural history," we have inherited, still intact, that Greek
sense of the word, and as is implied by the condition of objectivity that presides over those specific kinds of knowledge, the
truest history — "truest" in the Greek sense of *aletheia*: truth as

genuineness — would be the record that would make itself, without human mediation. Its author would be nature, or rather the principal agent or divinity ever present in nature — that abstract principle whose justification, in regard to the absolutely unbound future that sets it apart from the world of men, lies merely in its existence. Transferred to the sphere of myth, its figure would be Chronos, the divinity who produces sons, plagues, wars, and heroes — "history making" events — with the same indifference with which he devours them.

"History making events": no subterfuge of language is innocent, and yet none is entirely opaque. The physical analogy soon discloses its own limits. Physics entails a record of events — for instance, the flight of an arrow (as described by physical laws) — and yet we do not say that the flight of a particular arrow "made physics" more than any other, though the flight of one particular arrow and not another "made history" at the walls of Troy.

The presumed indifference of the "making" of history involves a paradox that resembles the subterfuge of Ulysses in his mystification of Polyphemus: *Udeis* is my name: I am he who does not exist. In this departure from the indissoluble vehicle that binds natural man with his name, Adorno and Horkheimer saw the beginning of the development of bourgeois consciousness. The *Odyssey* is not properly an epic but the first novel.

In the last book of Calvino's trilogy *Our Ancestors*, the inaugural hubris of Odysseus is enacted by the figure of the Non-Existent Knight. His armor is of spotless white. His coat of arms depicts a pair of stage curtains, opening into another pair, and so on, into infinity. His main virtue is exactitude, and his cause regulations. The only problem is that on parade he cannot lift his visor. When the Emperor presses compliance, he discovers that the armor is empty. "I do not exist," explains the Knight. "How can you then be here?" asks the Emperor. "By a sheer act of my will to serve."

Udeis/Odysseus inaugurates the strenuous destiny of Goethe's Hermann, and anticipates, in a different sense, the solipsistic wanderings of Childe Harold. He prefigures the main theme of romantic literature, the *Bildung*, the shaping or constructing of the self by design. The logical form implied by this theme is the form of teleology, the pure search for *telos*, perfection, indifferent to content and therefore essentially unfulfillable. Faust's challenge to Mephistopheles expresses the condition of time thus postulated: "If I ever beg the instant/'stay! thou art so beautiful!'/then canst thou load me with chains/ willingly my death I shall accept."

My name is *Udeis*. I do not exist, but *ich diene*. Such is the armor of power in the history of modern society. The figure of its presence, made structure, is the recurrent set of stage curtains opening into a stage within which myths and all narrative substance have dissolved. History, the witness of time, has finally no other object to witness than the blank mind of Chronos, his unbounded capacity for memory canceled by an equally unbounded capacity for forgetfulness. In the structure that fixes teleology into pure form, historic consciousness cancels itself within itself, concealing the power of memory to rescue *historical* events from oblivion, and setting oblivion against the discriminatory judgment that raises them above the flowing river of *physis*.

Romantic thought had conceived this highlighting power in terms of a figure: the subject is a lamp, the source of a sensibility that, by selective illumination, shapes the formless river into recognizable faces and objects. The figure is reminiscent of an older one: Plato's picture of the ideal as a fire projecting the procession of the nameless bodies that constitute the real into the shapes and shadows of mimetic appearance. But the evolution of the bourgeois conception of memory entails the neutralization of its critical potential, the taming of the fire of the ideal into the lamp of the subject. It construes historical discourse as *other* and yet *similar* to the discourse of physical science; physical laws resist the devouring power of time because they refer to events without according to them the condition of the singular — without recognizing in them a comparable ontological status to that which they themselves have as laws. In a similar manner the bourgeois subject construes memory, though still as criticism, as the capacity to establish itself *beyond* the reach of time. Thus in the same act of severance by which the subject cuts itself free from the river of *physis*, it establishes the ideal at a "meta-" level so that its critical power cancels itself within itself. Its *motto* is the figure depicted in the coat of arms of the Non-Existent Knight.

It is a recursive device similar to that of Tarsky's theory of truth, which, by postulating the semantic *nexus* of language in a metalanguage whose semantic *nexus* resides in still another metalanguage, resolves all semantic paradoxes by infinitely reproducing their internal structure.

In this construction necessity becomes pure *otherness* with respect to existence. Its figure is the song (*Some of These Days*) that the failed historian, Antoine Roquentin, plays again and again in Sartre's *La Nausée*, his talisman against the anguishing experience of the blind concatenation of immanent facts. Because it has a definite beginning and a definite end (as the *mechanism* of the phonograph demonstrates), the song has a shape, a recognizable *eidos* (form), within which the subject can recognize, as in a mirror, his own image as *being* — beyond existence. As memory. Memory as pure *durée*, other than time. Unattainable, *au delà — toujours au delà de quelque chose*. Projected into the perfection of accomplishment: pure *telos*.

And yet Roquentin's escape is not so much impossible — the scent of wood at the railway station, which in the last line of the novel announces with the imminent rain the unbroken tyranny of existence — as it is illusory: *telos* as pure form, the song contained within a beginning and an end, depends on the mechanical concatenation of movement of the phonograph. Time as pure *eidos* and time as brute fact are but two equivalent names for the same substance: the power of Chronos.

□

Sartre's figure of the melody on the phonograph, aesthetic *telos* as *other* than existence, has its origin in Kant's conception of aesthetic judgment. Writing at the end of the nineteenth century, Bernard Bosanquet recognized in that conception a decisive threshold in the maturity of modern man's consciousness. The role of the *Critique of the Faculty of Judgment* within the critical program tends to confirm this view. Having addressed himself to the two main themes of the Enlightenment, reason as a guide in the knowledge of the physical world and reason as a guide in ethics and politics, and aware that the two branches of his inquiry did not meet, Kant designed *The Critique of the Faculty of Judgment* as a keystone to the arch of critical reason. Criticism was to be thereby shaped into a coherent form — the *eidos* of man itself.

In this manner, according to Bosanquet, a development that had begun in classical Greece with the disturbing realization of the severance' of poetry from myth reached maturity only when, at the end of the Enlightenment, the domain of the aesthetic was conceived, with full theoretical awareness, as an autonomous domain: in Kant's formula, pure teleology, purposiveness without a purpose. In accordance with this formula Schiller could recognize the spirit of *paideia*, which had marked the Greek childhood of mankind, as a premonition of the age that was now to set man — modern man — in communion with the creative priniciple of the universe.

The autonomy of the aesthetic realm was thus the key both to the autonomous establishment of scientific reason, through a reflective examination of its own grounds, and to the assertion of that moral autonomy of man that the Enlightenment had sought and projected as political liberty. And although, later, at the peak of romanticism, the formula carried with it an undeniable measure of idealization and displacement with respect to the more concrete objectives of the preceding decades, and although it was by then already uncertain in which manner, or even whether, a new age would come to fulfill the hopes that the Revolution had left unfulfilled, its optimistic appeal for modern man was undeniable: utility free from the vulgarity of bourgeois interest; almost a pure perfume, and yet self-consistent and necessary. Truth as nothing but splendor — *pace* Aquinas's distinction between the splendor (Beauty) and the substance of Truth (with revelation at its core).

However, the idea could be expressed only in what, if read literally, was a paradox; in a sense, the semantic paradox in another form. The strategem of Odysseus: the name of my purpose is that I have no purpose (of my own). *Ich diene.*

The gap that the expression concealed under the perfume and splendor of the pure form of *telos* had already been exposed by the critical currents of the Enlightenment. The internal necessity of reason, the impulse that urged modern man not only to assert his own being in the form of a politically free subject, but also to attain the highest peaks of poetry and speculation, was irreconcilable with the necessity that ruled the succession of events in the world outside; and not only was he reminded of that blind necessity by the restraining power that it exerted upon his own flesh, he had also to formulate it as the only objective counterpart to reason itself, when reason was applied to its more immediate and legitimate aim, the modeling of the world of experience.

In a revealing passage of the *Critique of Pure Reason*, Kant gives a somber image of that gap:

> We have now not only traveled through the land of pure understanding, and carefully surveyed every part of it, but we have also measured its extent and assigned to everything its proper place. This land however is an island, and is enclosed by nature herself within unchangeable limits. It is the Land of Truth (an appealing name!); but a wide and stormy ocean surrounds it, the very seat of illusion, where many a fog bank, many an iceberg appears to the mariner, in his exploration, as New Land, and while inces-

santly deluding him with empty hopes, reduces him to adventures from which he can never desist, and yet which he can never bring to completion.[1]

From those shores bourgeois reason was never to depart with self-confidence. Four years after the publication of the *Critique of Pure Reason* Kant reviewed Herder's *Ideas on the Philosophy of the History of Mankind*. The appeal of history had never been as pervasive as it was in the Enlightenment. The crisis of the traditional metaphysical grounds from which institutions had received their justification opened the door to a search for their origins by means of which reason was expected to discover the principles of the moral and social realm. Yet in this very appeal, lurking behind the promise to lay open innumerable new lands to the survey of reason, Kant saw the futility of the attempt to ignore "that stormy ocean, the very seat of illusion" of which he had spoken. After the fruitless speculations of traditional metaphysics, historical relativism was only a confirmation of the impending doom of skepticism, still another aimless wandering for a reason that had lost the sense of necessity.

A few months before his review of Herder, Kant had considered the epistemological role of history in two short articles in which he stated for the first time the position he was to develop in the *Critique of Practical Reason*.[2] In contrast to those who sought to derive from history the justification of moral and social laws, Kant argued that historical discourse itself could only be justified in terms of what *ought to be*; and it was in this sense that the question of history became central to the critical program. Just as, in the *Critique of Pure Reason*, Kant had sought to reestablish the achievements of modern science deriving from the Newtonian revolution by critically examining its epistemological foundations, Kant sought now to reestablish the revolutionary social claims of the Enlightenment by a similar examination of its central moral and political themes, particularly as they had been stated by Rousseau.

In the first of these articles he writes: "The means that are available to Nature for the total completion of her plans reside in the very antagonisms that occur within society, however distant such an original cause may be from her aim to establish a regular

---

[1] *Kritik der reinen Vernunft*, B 294 – 295, A 235 – 236.
[2] "Idee zu einer allgemeinen Geschichte in Weltbürgerlichen Absicht" ("Ideas for a General History from a Cosmopolitan Point of View") and "Beantwortung der Frage: Was ist Aufklärung?" ("Answer to the Question: What Is the Enlightenment?"), both published in *Berlinische Monatsschrift*, November 1784 (385 – 411) and December 1784 (481 – 494) respectively.

order. By antagonisms I mean the antisocial sociability of men (*die ungesellige Geselligkeit der Menschen*)."[3] The foundations of the state of culture, whose realization gives meaning to history, are to be found in the interplay between, on the one hand, material necessity, " ... finding food, shelter, and defense, since she (Nature) gave him, instead of the horns of bulls, the claws of lions, and the teeth of dogs, nothing but his bare hands"[4] — and, on the other, the antisocial (and hardly less natural) impulses of men — greed, egotism, inclination to idleness. "There, the first true steps can be shown of the transition from barbarism to that state of culture in which the social value of men properly resides; thus gradually all talents were developed, tastes formed, and, through continued enlightenment, the beginnings of a manner of thought were established whereby a natural pre-disposition to make ethical distinctions developed into definite principles of practice, while a compulsory and pathological association was transformed into the moral totality of society. These antisocial qualities, which originate in the resistance confronted by anyone in the pursuit of his egotistical impulses, may be unattractive in themselves, but without them, and in an Arcadian life dominated by universal accord, peace, and mutual love, every talent would remain buried in its own seed. Men, being as good-natured as the sheep they pastured, would not assign to their own existence any higher value than to that of those very sheep; they would thus fail to fulfill the unfulfilled aim of creation in regard to its destiny as rational Nature."[5]

The function of the Enlightenment as a historical threshold[6] — the cumulative result of a long effort of "continued enlightenment," "development of talent," and "formation of taste" — resides precisely in the fulfillment of that aim: the culmination of Nature in autonomous reason. "The Enlightenment is the end of the self-inflicted minority of Mankind. By minority I mean the inability to use one's own understanding without someone else's guidance. Such minority is self-inflicted when it springs not so much from a want of understanding itself as from a want of the resolution and courage to use it without being guided by somebody else. *Sapere aude!* Have the courage to avail thyself of thy own understanding! This is the motto of the Enlightenment."[7]

---

[3] "Idee zu einer allgemeinen Geschichte ...," 392.
[4] Ibid., 390.
[5] Ibid., 393.
[6] "Was ist Aufklärung?", 480 ("Do we live in an enlightened age? No, we live in the Age of Enlightenment.")

It is also the basis for the justification of all civil liberties in the religious and political spheres, as well as in the sphere of pure thought. This is the central argument of the second article published by Kant in the *Berlinische Monatsschrift*. For him (as for Rousseau), the justification of the social order has to find its way between the conflicting demands of freedom and necessity, between the right to choose one's own destiny without external determination and the duty of obedience to laws. For both Kant and Rousseau, this depends upon the justification of the possibility of a transmutation or continuity between these opposite poles. The key to the Enlightenment (indeed, the culmination of the movement of rational humanism that had begun in Italy in the fourteenth century) was the belief that the real meaning of history lay in the passage from the pole of experience, or *de facto*, to the pole of reason, or *de jure*.

But while for Rousseau the transmutation runs from the pole of nature to the pole of legality — by renouncing natural freedom and throwing it into the pool of *la volunté Générale*, the individual receives it back transmuted, justified, and effectively enhanced, as political liberty — for Kant it runs in the opposite direction: the legality that becomes patent in the social order (and allows, therefore, the very thought of political liberty) is the purest manifestation of the *same* legality that lends its structure to the impulses, trends, and patterns without which experience would never take for us the shape of nature (and which makes memory, indeed recognition, possible).

This, in a different guise, is the inversion that Kant called his "Copernican revolution." The final achievement of that long effort toward gradual enlightenment of which history consists, the justification of legality entails, since the whole domain of legality is postulated to be coextensive with that of reason, the reflective application of reason to itself and upon its very center: a trial in which, in terms of the judicial metaphor that runs through the preface to the *Critique of Reason*, reason is both judge and accused.

The accusation springs from the age itself. It is made manifest by its indifference toward metaphysics. This indifference is not the result of levity, but of the mature judgment of the age,[8] which does not let itself be hindered any longer by illusory knowledge. Therefore the Copernican revolution is only the summing-up of the main critical forces of the Enlightenment;

---

[7] Ibid., 481.
[8] " ... die Wirkung nicht des Leichtsinns, sondern der gereiften Urteilskraft der Zeitalters," *KRV*, A, XI.

what it postulates is only a generalization of the critical method that had proved so successful in those sciences ("Mathematics, the Science of Nature," etc.), which by finding their own autonomous domains had established themselves upon "solid foundations."[9]

Hume had already made "the application of experimental philosophy to moral subjects" the aim of his philosophical program. "It is impossible," he writes, "to tell what changes and improvements we might make in these sciences were we thoroughly acquainted with the extent and force of human understanding.... Here then is the only expedient from which we can hope for success in our philosophical researches, to leave the tedious lingering method which we have hitherto followed, and instead of taking now and then a castle or village on the frontier, to march up directly to the capital or center of these sciences, to human nature itself."[10]

But the conquest of that "capital center" entailed for Kant, as a consequence of his Copernican revolution, the inversion of the approach of the Enlightenment. Against his original intention, Hume had shown that the attempt to extend the *method* of experimental science to the analysis of human reason was to result not only in a failure to justify our knowledge of the traditional content matter of philosophy — "Logics, Morals, Aesthetics, and Politics," which comprehend "almost everything which it can in any way import us to be acquainted with"[11] — but also, by a total reverse of fortune, in destroying the justification of our knowledge of the content of the natural sciences themselves, whose progress had inspired the program of the Enlightenment. Thus Kant, who saw in the salvaging of this new content the crucial test for modern reason (though not its most important goal), took the opposite approach: to make the legality of the sciences of nature dependent upon the specificity of their approach. It was not the empiricism of those sciences that had to be extended into a universal principle, but the condition of autonomy that they illustrated. Their specificity depended upon the fact that they aimed at determining what *in experience* had truth value; there was to be, thus, no transfer of method — even less of content — from that direction. On the other hand, the ground thus established for modern science was to find its symmetrical counterpart and its guarantee in the autonomy of reason when it established the grounds of legality *in itself* (that is, when *free from*

---

[9] Ibid.
[10] D. Hume, *A Treatise of Human Nature* ... (London, 1739), Introduction.
[11] Ibid.

experience), in the domain of morals.

The sense in which that contrast could be understood as a continuity, and the intrinsic legality of reason could be brought to warrant the laws of Nature, did not become clear for Kant until later in the development of his program, when he faced the critique of the aesthetic domain, which was also a critique of the *idea* of Nature. There he found in the traditional concept of the unity of the aesthetic object the perfect illustration of the synthesis of experience and necessity: a synthesis where necessity and permanence were phenomenally inherent in, and not superfluously added to, the flow of experience itself (as, for Hume, was the case for any idea that entailed a component of permanence, substance, or necessity as its object). Negatively also, the autonomy of the aesthetic domain became a condition of the rationality of science, and Kant, as a critic of the sentimentalization of natural science that was so frequent in his age, brought to its logical conclusion the critical stance of the Enlightenment toward religion. Religious illusion — finally even the illusions of *Emile*'s natural religiosity — was prompted, above all, by the assumption held by so many eighteenth-century "Platonists" and sentimental idealists that the aesthetic and the epistemic domains were essentially the same.

Kant's Copernican revolution, in its opposition to Rousseau (which parallels its opposition to Hume), entails the promise of a new formulation, in reverse, of that synthesis of freedom and legality that the Enlightenment felt to be its own specific aim. Rousseau's scheme, indebted as it still was to the classicist nostalgia for a Golden Age, allowed, properly speaking, no place for history. Even if Rousseau allowed for the idea of revolution as an abstract idea, even if he conceived of the birth of a *corps politique* as a strictly legal event, conventional in its nature, these phenomena were seen as arising from primitive necessity with the suddenness of a natural cataclysm — a jump into darkness (as Fichte was to characterize revolution in the light of the French experience). Because the clauses of the social contract "can all be reduced to one: the total alienation of every associated member, with all his rights, to the community as a whole," and because therefore the *new* State can suffer no degree of overlap with the state of nature, the convention ceases entirely to exist once it is violated and everyone "takes up again his natural freedom, while losing the *conventional* freedom for which his natural freedom had been renounced."[12]

For Kant, who stood firmly on the side of modernism,

---

[12] J. J. Rousseau, *Du contrat social,* ch. VI.

and aloof from the classical tradition, such a "state of nature," even if garlanded with the wreaths of Arcadia, was nothing but barbarism — *Rohigkeit*. Enlightenment could thus only be the result of history, a progressive application of the critical power of reason to both belief and custom, such as finally to dispel dogmatism in science — where it took the shape of metaphysical opinion — and in religion, morals, and politics. The decisive threshold would consist in the application of that critical power to reason itself, thus dissolving all metaphysical illusion and, by the same token, all forms of tyranny.

□

Considering how they catalyzed and brought the critical threads of the Enlightenment within the framework of a systematic critique, the two articles of 1784 were seminal contributions to the new awareness of history that marked the change from the age of classicism to the modern era. As Ernst Cassirer writes, "It may seem at first sight that these articles are only short occasional pieces; however, they already contain the bases for the new conceptions developed by Kant concerning the nature of history and the State. It is therefore proper to attribute to these apparently unimportant studies a significance that, for the future trajectory of German idealism, is hardly less than that of the *Critique of Pure Reason* within its own domain."[13]

One possibly unexpected direction that the trajectory of German idealism took during the nineteenth century may be related to these articles. The voluntaristic conception of consciousness that flourished during its late phase in the writings of Nietzsche and Kierkegaard had its origins in Schopenhauer's reading of Kant, and the tone of their reading was certainly in accordance with the motto attributed by Kant to the Enlightenment. *Sapere aude!*, lucidity as the fruit of courage. There was, it is true, too much of the circumstance and climate of romanticism for this view to coincide with the intentions of Kant's philosophy taken as a whole. However, there was even in Kant an element of ambiguity that made this late-romantic position possible. Since the meaning of history resided in the progress of reason as enlightenment, and Kant believed that progress could only be defined in terms of moral, not of scientific, knowledge, reason itself seemed to depend upon the operation of the will.

[13] *Kants Leben und Lehre*. Cassirer also remarks that Kant's "Idee zu einer allgemeinen Geschichte ... " was the first writing by Kant that Schiller read and that it brought him to study Kant's philosophy.

Kant's inquiry into the principle of legality took a direction that was not the symmetrical opposite of Rousseau's naturalism. Where, for Rousseau, the passage *from nature to legality* was one single generative transmutation, Kant made a distinction of levels. He conceived of this passage as an analytical regression (*from the legality of reason to nature*) at an epistemological, and only at an epistemological, level; at the ontic level it was still nature that, for Kant as for Rousseau, generated legality. It was this later process — history proper — that brought to fulfillment the aim — *Zweck* — of Nature herself, in that Nature demanded to be rational. What is more, such a demand expressed its ontic unfulfillment, or "void" — *das Leere der Schöpfung*: literally, "the void of (or in) creation" — and was therefore irrenunciable.

The two levels differed from each other in their manners of articulation: at the ontic level, reason would be founded (negatively) in nature, where it would appear as "a void"; epistemologically, it would bring about its own foundation by an analytical regress that would lead to the discovery of its own limits. With respect to the historical genesis of society, that ontic "void" would become manifest in those antisocial impulses that constituted its very ground. But what Kant expressed as a brilliant paradox — the "antisocial sociability of men"[14] — concealed a fundamental ambiguity. Having assumed the distinction between the ontic and the epistemological levels, the "void," while belonging to both, appeared to do so with mutually contradictory implications. While in regard of the ontological constitution of nature, legality would find its ground in the filling of that void, at the level of epistemological analysis, the void would appear as an inherent epistemic *emptiness* of legality — the realization that knowledge without experience has no content.

The ambiguity deriving from that duality of levels corresponds to the ambiguity with which Kant assumes that reason is *other* than nature. On the one hand — and this is the sense in which the legality of reason comes to be established by history — the "otherness" of reason consists in the fact that its object lies in the conquest of that which in nature appears as a "void" — "barbarism." In this sense the ground of reason lies in a "meta-" domain, where "meta-" is construed as "beyond," like a land or domain of which we have no experience because it is (as yet) unvisited. But the radicalism of his critique of metaphysics (a domain of knowledge to which the Greek preposition "meta-"

---

[14] Cf. the also paradoxical formulation of the aesthetic as an autonomous domain: *zwecklos Zwecklichkeit*. But here the paradox is harsher: the prefix *un-* in *ungesellige* entails an element of active opposition, and not mere absence.

seems to apply, according to the classical tradition, in exactly this latter sense) prompted Kant to conceive the otherness of reason somehow in the manner in which we nowadays understand the otherness of a metalanguage with respect to its object-language, where "meta-" is construed as "above" (to follow the spatial metaphor carried by the Greek *ethymos*, like a cloud rather than like another province on the surface of the earth).[15]

The trajectory of German idealism (and of critical thought later in our century) was marked by this conflation between on the one hand the derivation of legality from epistemological analysis, and on the other the subrogation of a metaphysical by a historical ground for legality. History, seen as the continuation of natural processes at their own level, has become a substitute for metaphysics in the task of constructing reason, while on the other hand the reflective task of epistemological analysis has come to be seen as identical to this construction.

At the end, coming back to Kant in full circle — but, as in all reenactments, presupposing an opposite perspective to that of the original, so that the problematic conceptions within which Kant struggled have come to be accepted as unquestioned postulates — that trajectory culminates in the total identity of *Grund* and *Grenze*, "foundation" and "boundary." The application of that postulate as a methodological absolute resulted first in the divorce of the "science of nature" from the "science of culture." Then, as these neo-Kantian bases developed into the epistemological formalism of the avant-gardes of our century, an infinite regress ensued, whereby culture came to be seen only in the refraction of countless "autonomous" structures, and history to elude the grasp of any firm conception. For instance, linguistics, which has acted as one of the major exemplary guides of this trend, illustrates the rise of a taxonomical manner of thought to such a point of dominance that any historical approach to language has become practically impossible.

This manner of thought can be traced back to a reductionist dissolution of the effort of the Enlightenment to reconcile the three main philosophical themes of classical humanism: nature, progress, and knowledge as *speculum* of the world. For

---

[15] This is entailed in Kant's very carefully construed distinction between (his own) "transcendental" and the (traditional metaphysical) "transcendent" use of "the idea of reason." For Kant all objects of the understanding must conceivably be *given* in (physical) experience. *Physis* is then taken as a closed totality, and the "transcendental system" that he proposes in lieu of traditional ("transcendent") metaphysics contains the key to the closure of *Physis* very much as, according to contemporary formal logic, any given object-language is taken as a closed totality, and the key to its closure made to reside in a corresponding metalanguage.

the development of the last of these themes the philosophers of the Enlightenment had found increasingly abundant material, not only in the advances of the natural sciences, but also in the widening diversity of social institutions and human mores available to observation. Unraveling that which was constant and stable from that which was transient and capricious, they had formed the notion of a principle of *order*, manifest in the universality of mathematical formulae, when applied to natural phenomena, as well as in the concordance of "good" institutions, taste, and moral sentiments among different nations, and they came to see this order as the fruit of a mirrorlike mimesis of nature by reason, a reflection distilled by criticism, which was itself based upon the power of reason to reflect upon itself (although it was only with Kant that the full implications of this last condition were realized). But while, because of its direction, that criticism could be linked with the development of progress, this latter theme carried with it a conception of reason as *constituting* the ideal against the obstacles raised by natural forces, and this active ontic role, derived from the Platonic tradition, was incompatible with the essentially passive conception of the mind as a pure mirror — of whatever there might be in the world — and itself devoid of any ontic substance. The dismissal of all "ontological commitments" in contemporary thought has made this tension meaningless. From the conceptions of reason as progress and reason as mimesis, the epistemological formalism of our century retained only their more abstract and immanent features. Playing the passive conception of knowledge as a mirror against the ontological activism implied in the demand for progress, and the active conception of reason as a constitutive principle against the epistemological transcendence implied in the demand for truth, formalism has come to postulate the identity of the constitutive and the reflective roles of reason, on the grounds that they both express its self-immanence, and, since this immanence can only be conceived negatively, it has come to reduce the triad of classical philosophy to a simple opposition where nature, existence, and necessity are immediately negated as *alien* by culture, form, and arbitrariness: the polarity expressed by Sartre by the figure of the melody in *La Nausée*, and as developed by the late epigones of French phenomenology.

□

Even in Kant's program the conflation between the epistemological and the ontological levels tends to define reason (form, structure) as pure *otherness* with respect to existence. Since

37

the third *Critique* was not meant to study a third field or class of objects, the duality form-existence, which subtends the critical program, is made patent in the opposition between the first and the second *Critiques*. The study of the field of science, the epistemic objects of which are "concepts," is set against the study of the field of ethics, the epistemic objects of which are "ideas." Reason is, in the first, applied to experience, to which it is other, in the second to itself as pure otherness. In the first, reason, concerned with the legality of what exists, reveals itself inescapably incomplete; in the second, where it appears complete and self-consistent, its concern is with the legality of what does not exist: the map of possibility. Moral self-determination, the criterion that marks the historical appearance of enlightened man, entails the self-consistent realization of full legality; but since full legality, thus considered, extends beyond the domains of experience, the critical function of moral (that is, complete) reason is to shape the domain of possibility by marking its bounds — just as the critical function of "pure" (that is, incomplete) reason shapes the domains of intelligibility by marking the bounds of the understanding. Thus when Kant rejects "the ontological ideal of perfection ... as a rational ground for morality," his argument is that this idea is "so empty, so undetermined, that it cannot serve the function of extracting from the immeasurable field of possible reality the maximum sum that agrees with us."[16] Within the framework of classical philosophy the idea of absolute perfection, as well as the idea of absolute truth, would have been either asserted by the idealists, or denied by the empiricists, as belonging to a transcendent ontological domain. Kant's "transcendental" idealism dodges this dilemma by attributing to reason, in the exercise of its critical function, the power to determine, within the "immeasurability" of such a transcendent ontological domain, a commensurate field, the "maximum sum which agrees with us."

The radical departure intended by the Copernican revolution extends to "practical" as well as to "pure" reason. But their analogy in this respect contains the notion of a progression and therefore a dissimilarity. The central criterion of the Copernican revolution, the concept of *agreeing with us*, carries with it a teleological implication.[17] It is therefore only as "practical rea-

---

[16] " ... um in der unermesslichen Felds möglicher Realität die für uns schickliche grösste Summe auszufinden." *Grundlegung zur Metaphysik der Sitten*, 91 – 92. Cf. also E. Cassirer, op. cit., commenting on another passage of the same work: "The peculiar and specific 'reality' of the idea of freedom consists precisely in that, because it does not shy at the postulate of the apparently impossible, it closes in itself the circle of the possible."

Francisco Goya, Capricho No. 13, *1799*

son" — concerned with the teleology of human action — that reason achieves the plenitude of its critical function. This asymmetry concurs with, and in a sense contradicts, the analogy that links the first and the second *Critiques*. Their mutual contrast becomes apparent in the prerequisite for the principle of moral self-determination. The *sapere aude!*, upon which the autonomy of practical reason is based has, as far as pure reason is concerned, only a negative content: the determination of that which it is *impossible* to know.

□

The fissure that thus underlies the development of the critical program derives from the ambiguity with which it conceives of the domain of the ontological as "guaranteed" by that of the epistemological — from the conflation between "foundation" and "boundary." If the *Critique of the Faculty of Judgment* could do no more than attempt to heal that fissure by means of the paradoxical notion of "purposiveness without a purpose," it was also with paradoxical arguments that Kant confronted the problem of the ontological foundation of reason in the first *Critique*.

Toward the end of the Analytic of Principles, when he develops the long-expected "refutation of Idealism," thus finally establishing the legality for enlightened reason to possess the fruits of eighteenth-century empirical science, Kant has to deal with the last triad of the table of categories — possibility, existence, necessity — considering specifically their use in synthetic judgments, i.e. judgments involving actual experience. This entails a problem that Kant avoided when he examined these categories in the Analytic of Concepts from a purely logical point of view, but which has to be confronted now, namely that of their *extensio*. The question he asks is "whether the field of possibility is larger than that of reality, and this, in its turn, larger than that of necessity." In view of the structure of the triad, as it appears in the table of categories, it would seem that the answer to this question should be affirmative; since, as each category seems to add something to the *intensio* of the preceding one, so its *extensio* has to be, correspondingly, reduced. Kant, however, defends the opposite. This is his argument: "It would seem as if one should make the sum of the possible [*die Zahl des Möglichen*] overlap and extend beyond that of the real[18] (because something has

---

[17] The German term *schicklich*, which Kant uses in the quotation above, while linking connotatively with the classical moral concept of *decus*, involves in its *ethymos* the teleological concept of *destination*.

to be added to the former in order to constitute the latter). But such an addition to the possible is inconceivable, for that which would thus be added to it would be impossible."[19]

The awkwardness of the argument is striking; its wording entails an equivocation that can be made patent if one reproduces its logical form in this example: "It would seem as if one should make the sum of /the organic/ overlap and extend beyond that of/the animal,/ because something has to be added to the former in order to constitute the latter. But such an addition to/the organic/is inconceivable, for that which should thus be added to it would be/inorganic./" The expression "that which should be added to (the possible)" — *was über das Mögliche zugesetzt werden sollte* — must be construed as "added to the *extensio* of /the possible/" for the conclusion that it is / impossible / to be valid, while the question asked in the preceding premise concerns the notion of "adding to the *intensio* of / the possible /"; the conclusion that it would be "impossible" does not therefore follow.

What Kant means can only be adumbrated by the context. The reader has to remember that Kant is not dealing here with "possibility" and "existence" as pure logical concepts, but with their use in "synthetic judgments," i.e., with respect to experience. From the point of view that he has previously established — that of transcendental idealism — such a synthetic function involves the use of categories in relation to the interconnectedness of experience. From this perspective, anything that can be connected with a *particular* (sensorial) experience is not only possible, but also real (even if not immediately perceived), and that which can be connected only with purely possible (therefore totally indeterminate) experience is not possible in *any* (particular) connection. What Kant wants to say is simply that the notion of pure *logical* possibility (as opposed to the notion of *empirical* possibility, i.e., compatibility with a set of *definite* empirical circumstances), is not amenable to empirical use, but belongs to reason alone, and passes beyond the bounds of the island surveyed by the first *Critique*.

However, the apparently unnecessary difficulty encountered in the formulation of the argument betrays a profound difficulty that is central to the position of transcendental idealism. For it is only if one accepts that position that the restriction of possibility — and the other categories of modality, existence, and

---

[18] Kant uses here the term "real" [*wirklich*]. In the table of categories he uses "existence" [*Dasein*].

[19] *KRV*, A 231, B 284.

41

necessity — argued for in the *Critique of Reason* becomes plausible. And then if one proposes to distinguish between possibility and existence along the lines thus suggested, the distinction between possibility and necessity becomes problematic.

This can be demonstrated by another difficulty in another passage of the *Critique*, which is closely connected with the one just discussed. The empirical use of categories entails what Kant calls their "schematism," i.e., the manner in which concepts informed by them relate to particular objects in the manifold of experience so as to bring about its interconnectedness. Kant discusses the schematism of categories in the first chapter of the Analytic of Principles. When he deals with the triad of modality, the schematism of existence is characterized as "existence in a determined time" — *das Dasein in einer bestimmten Zeit*; that of possibility as the "concordance of the synthesis of different representations with the conditions of time in general" — *mit den Bedingungen der Zeit überhaupt*; that of necessity as "the existence of an object in all time" — *das Dasein eines Gegenstandes zu aller Zeit.*"[20] The sense of these distinctions when seen in the context of the general principles of transcendental idealism — especially with respect to the status of time as an *a priori* form of experience — seems clear enough. Again it is the wording that seems unfortunate, for the distinction between "time in general" and "all time" is uncomfortably vague.

The impression that both these passages give is that Kant runs into unexpected and somehow minor difficulties because he rushes through the argument — this is apparent even in terms of style;[21] but although the *Critique of Pure Reason* bears many traces of the mood of urgency under which it was written, Kant's curtness in this particular context suggests that more specific motives were here at work.

Given the character of his particular philosophical environment, Kant could hardly be unaware of the fact that the categories of possibility, existence, and necessity were, for the classical philosophical tradition, pervaded with ontological implications. In placing them, as one more triad, within the table of categories, alongside categories — such as singularity, plurality, and totality — which were of a strict logico-formal nature,

---

[20] *KRV*, A 144 – 145, B 184.

[21] For instance, the schemata of existence and necessity are each dealt with in a single-sentence paragraph: in the first edition the sentence corresponding to "necessity" omits the verb *ist*. This was added in the second edition. More revealing is Kant's terminological indecision between "reality" — *Wirklichkeit* — and "existence" — *Dasein* — which appears at first sight due to purely stylistic reasons.

Kant was taking sides with respect to the crisis that in his time surrounded that tradition, particularly regarding the difficult question of the relation of formal disciplines (mathematics and logics) to metaphysics. Kant's impatience betrays his feeling that any extended discussion of the categories of modality could run dangerously close to the central nerve of the modernity of his position.

The last paragraph of the section entitled "Postulates of Empirical Thought" — which is devoted to the function of the categories of modality in the "synthesis of experience" — contains in fact a lucid statement of the peculiar status of these categories:

> The principles of modality, however, are not objectively synthetical, because the predicates of possibility, reality, and necessity do not augment in the least the concepts on which they are predicated, in the sense that they contribute nothing in particular to the representation of the object. Inasmuch as they are nevertheless still synthetical, they are so only subjectively; that is, they submit to the concept of a certain (real) thing, of which otherwise they say nothing, the very faculty of knowledge in which the concept originates and has its seat.

That this restrictive conception was incompatible with the ambitious aims of the critical program is something that becomes apparent even within the scope of the *Critique of Pure Reason*. For instance, in the Dialectic, when he discusses the resolution of the "dynamic" antinomies, Kant refers, as Strawson has noted, to a conception of a necessity that has little to do with the empirically bounded conception previously delineated in the Analytic of Principles.

□

Since the difficulties commented upon above occur in relation to the synthetic function of the categories of modality with respect to experience, it should be expected that they have to do with Kant's conception of time. When he discusses, in the context of the Analytic of Principles,[22] the principle of the per-

---

[22] The context is extremely significant: this is the first of the three principles stated under the title "Analogies of Experience"; the other two are the principle of causation and the principle of correspondence between action and reaction. Kant is dealing here, in a sense, with the culmination of the *Critique*, its closest point of

manence of substance, he says, "Permanence is the ultimate expression of time.... For change does not affect time itself, but only the phenomena in time.... If succession was to be attributed to time itself, then it would be necessary to think of another time within which this succession would be possible."[23]

The passage has strangely archaic, almost Eleatic resonances. Or, to look for a closer parallel, one is reminded of the Leibnizian conception of time — in analogy with space — as a sort of infinite container. And yet, since it would be hard to find in the philosophical traditions more extreme examples than these of an ontological commitment to transcendental idealism, such as Kant wanted to avoid, this conception of time seems to be at odds with the dissolution of metaphysics, which is the stated aim of the whole critical program. If one bears in mind this aim, the passage should be interpreted as a key case of the conflation between the two senses of "meta-" that I have described above — where "meta-" as in "metaphysical" is dissolved into "meta-" as in "metalanguage."

But then if time is to be considered in this manner, as a pure *a priori* form, as a frame beyond (and above) the contents of experience, there is no way to distinguish between "all the time" — *alle Zeit* — and "time in general" — *Zeit überhaupt* (even if taken as "any time"). Both expressions can only denote the *whole extent of the pure form of time*, for *any* distinctive "mark" that would enable us to refer to *any* moment as a *single* point in opposition to the whole could only belong to the *content* of that form — changes *within* time — and not to the form itself. It becomes therefore strictly impossible, if one assumes such a conception of time, to distinguish, as Kant proposes, between the schemata of possibility and necessity. On the other hand, the schema of existence appears, as in a flat silhouette, in the nonmediated contrast between that which belongs to the "here and now" (the contents of experience) and that which belongs to the frame or "meta-" level.

□

By beginning the *Phenomenology of the Spirit* with a critique of the "here and now" as *the* ultimate and nonmediated ontological criterion, Hegel recognized the central difficulty that had

convergence to Newton's physics. But it is also, precisely because of this, the point where the ontological purport of his philosophy demands to be expressed in more precise terms.
[23] *KRV*, A 183, B 226.

hindered the critical program. For it is precisely Kant's belief that there is no other ontological vector but the effect that the "here and now" introduces as a wedge within the frame of *a priori* forms, which generates the nonmediated contradiction he encounters between knowledge as experience of the *given* and knowledge as the activity of reason,[24] knowledge of what "is-there" and knowledge of what "ought-to-be."

There is no possibility of synthesis, then, no hope of establishing the unity of reason, other than that which is contained within the *focus*, which alone gives sense to the "here and now": the subject *for* whom they are precisely *this* "here" and *this* "now." The conclusion of the Analytic of Principles, that in the schemata of modality, including necessity, there occurs no objective but merely a subjective synthesis, reveals all its inescapable force. And then the ontological synthesis that practical reason demands in its projection toward that which "ought to be," the synthesis of the ideal, cannot have any more objectivity than a mirage. There will always remain, underlying that synthesis, the irreconcilable opposition between the epistemic and the epistemological, between reason as inhabiting the world, and reflexive reason judging (and only that) itself. It is precisely by means of the image of the mirror that Kant describes the "transcendental" operation of ideas in the domain of practical reason:

> ... to direct the understanding toward a certain aim, toward which all the guiding lines of its rules converge as if into a point. This point, although it is only an idea (*focus imaginarius*), i.e., a point from which the concepts of the understanding do not really proceed, since it lies beyond the bounds of any possible experience, fulfills nevertheless the function of endowing these concepts with the greatest unity in relation to their greatest extension. From this precisely originates the mirage effect [*Täuschung*] that those guiding lines are released by an object that lies outside the field of empirical cognition (just as objects reflected in a mirror appear to be behind it).

This passage is at the beginning of the "Appendix to the Dialectic," a section of extraordinary importance, historically

---

[24] See *KRV*, A 836, B 864: "All knowledge is either historical or rational. Historical knowledge is *cognito ex datis*, rational knowledge *cognito ex principiis*." It is symptomatic that, when he opposes it to rational knowledge, Kant chooses to call empirical knowledge *historical* (unintentionally reviving the original Greek meaning of the term).

[25] *KRV*, A 644, B 672.

because it was to provide the link for the development of Hegel's philosophy, and systematically because it links the architecture of the *Critique of Pure Reason* (and particularly the triadic organization of the table of categories) with the central theme of the *Critique of Practical Reason*. The mirage mechanism responsible for the production of the "subjective synthesis" that we have found in the categories of modality is also responsible for the appearance of the "objective unity" of moral ideas. Kant's optical simile could be followed down to its detail: the point of convergence (*focus imaginarius*) toward which the regulative (and normative) lines of the ideal point, the domain where its objects appear to be, is, in truth, nothing but the symmetrical counterfield to the field of the eye (the subject) itself, the domain where he would be if he could really see such objects.

It has to be remarked that, however subjective it may be, the synthetic function of ideas is nonetheless inescapable — just as the eye cannot prevent itself seeing the objects *behind* the surface of the mirror. At the beginning of the Dialectic, Kant, referring to Plato as a precedent for his own use of the term "idea," comments, " ... since, while experience provides us in that which concerns nature with the relevant guidelines and is the source of truth, in that which concerns ethical norms experience is (unfortunately) the mother of error, and nothing could be more reprehensible than to deduce from, or to attempt to reduce to *what is done*, that which *I ought to do*."[26]

But the terms themselves of the antithesis — the subjective necessity of what "I ought to do" and the objective synthesis of "what is done" (which social experience provides me) — suggest that the necessity of the ideal is, strictly speaking, absent (and unattainable) from the sphere of nature, including human nature and its development into social institutions. The implications of the antithesis are clear in respect of the ontological status of moral norms, even when Kant sets himself pugnaciously in their defense. Two pages before the quoted passage he says, "The Platonic Republic has become the proverbial example of a chimerical perfection such as can only exist in the brain of the idle thinker.... But we would do better to follow up such lines of thought, and strive (where that admirable man leaves us without assistance) to bring it into a clearer light, rather than fling it aside as useless, with the very miserable and pernicious excuse that it is unfeasible."[27]

---

[26] *KRV*, A 318 – 319, B 375; *"was ich tun soll ... was getan wird."* The italics are Kant's.
[27] *KRV*, A 316, B 372 – 373.

Thus ideas are unfeasible — and yet it is only in them that necessity appears in its purest form. And the gap between *cognito ex datis* and *cognito ex principiis*, between that which is and that which ought to be, is unbridgeable, as it is impossible to embrace in a single glance the past and the future — and history, therefore, as intelligible succession.

The failure that the *Critiques* conceal within their spectacular architecture is revealed, as sentiment, in their rhetorical grain: " ... the very miserable and pernicious excuse of its unfeasibility ... "

The romantic and pugnacious color of the adjectives springs from the very same source as the melancholic lament of the mariner, condemned never to leave the shores of the island "surrounded by stormy oceans," never ceasing to be tempted by the mirages of unattainable Lands of Promise.

A deep resonance links the strategem of Ulysses with the impatient shortcuts — "purposiveness without purpose" — that mark the apex of bourgeois modernity. If Kant's conception of necessity reveals its insufficiency precisely in relation to his conception of time, it is this conception of time that — in the deduction of the Categories — Pure Reason uses as cement for the construction of the *subject*, in the same movement by which it sets itself up, through critical examination, as a frame or stage within which the plots of history are to be contained.

It is also the same conception that makes time — as the *a priori* form of sensibility — the *locus* of the brute facts of experience.

Time as pure eidos and time as brute fact are but two equivalent names for the same substance: the fear of Chronos.

It is the fear that the light tamed in the lamp might become again the fire in the cavern, and that the dark body of necessity might become visible, lit by another fire, in the propagation of fire from the other side.

It is also the fear of Zeus, the initiator of history.

SATURNE OU LE TEMS.

Le Corbusier, study sketch for the cover of Vers une Architecture, *originally to be titled* Architecture ou Révolution, *1922 or 1923*

Introduction

In the essay that follows, Fredric Jameson presents a critique of the writings of the Italian Marxist architectural historian
Manfredo Tafuri — in particular Tafuri's seminal and influential
book *Architecture and Utopia*, first published in Italian in 1973.
Unlike most analyses of Tafuri's work in the English-speaking
world (which tend to be either explications or outright rejections),
Jameson's article situates Tafuri's writing in a broader ideological
and historical context.

Beginning with a discussion of Tafuri's historiographic
approach, Jameson distinguishes the architectural historian's
Marxism from more "humanist" or "utopian" interpretations
(such as those of Herbert Marcuse and Henri Lefèbvre) and compares *Architecture and Utopia* to two other dialectical histories of
artistic fields that Jameson considers of comparable intellectual
intensity and achievement, Theodor Adorno's *Philosophy of Modern Music* (1949) and Roland Barthes's *Writing Degree Zero* (1953).
These three texts, Jameson claims, depend upon a vision of
necessity that results ultimately in narrative closure, "a blank
wall against which history cannot move." The contradictions
potently revealed by each of these studies — the fatal collapse of
aesthetic utopianism in its confrontation with material conditions
— necessarily determine an end to the future of each of their
respective aesthetic fields, and by extension, an abolition of
effective action and values in the realm of culture at large.
Jameson asserts that this closure, though a product of
method — dialectical historiography — may also, unfortunately,
be read as ideological; it may be linked, in fact, to the all-encom-
passing, systematic nature of late multinational capitalism. The
very totality of this system, marked by its global control, has
resulted in an insistence among many Marxists that socialist revolution is impossible until capitalism has exhausted itself worldwide. The only revolution is a global revolution. This position
Jameson associates with Tafuri's assertion that no qualitative
change in architecture, no "class architecture," can precede a
revolutionary transformation of the social order.

While fully acknowledging the pervasiveness of late capitalism, Jameson outlines an alternative position. He opposes
Tafuri's "pessimistic" assessment to what he calls a
"neo-Gramscian" view, which proposes the possibility of building enclaves — whether material or ideological — of revolutionary transformation in the present.

Finally, and perhaps most controversial to architects, Jameson compares Tafuri's stark and negative perspective to Robert Venturi's aesthetic of contradiction and fragmented chaos.

Mary McLeod

Architecture and the
Critique of Ideology

Fredric Jameson

How can space be "ideological"? Only if such a question is possible and meaningful — leaving aside the problem of meaningful *answers* to it — can any conceptions or ideals of non-ideological, transfigured, utopian space be developed. The question has itself tended to be absorbed by naturalistic or anthropological perspectives, most often based on conceptions of the human body, notably in phenomenology. The body's limits but also its needs are then appealed to as ultimate standards against which to measure the relative alienation of older commercial or industrial spaces, of the overwhelming sculptural monuments of the International Style, or else of the postmodernist "megastructure." Yet arguments based on the human body are fundamentally ahistorical, and involve premises about some eternal "human nature" concealed within the seemingly "verifiable" and scientific data of physiological analysis. If the body is in reality a social body, if therefore there exists no pre-given human body as such, but rather the whole historical range of social experiences of the body, the whole variety of bodily norms projected by a series of distinct historical "modes of production" or social formations, then the "return" to some more "natural" vision of the body in space projected by phenomenology comes to seem ideological, when not nostalgic. But does this mean that there are no limits to what the body, socially and historically, can become, or to the kind of space to which it can be asked to "adapt"?

Yet if the body ceases to be the fundamental unit of spatial analysis, at once the very concept of space itself becomes problematic: what space? The space of rooms or individual buildings? Or the space of the very city fabric itself in which those buildings are inserted, and against whose perceptual background my experience of this or that local segment is organized? Yet the city, however it is construed, is space-in-totality; it is not given in advance as an object of study or analysis, after the fashion of the constructed building. (Perhaps even the latter is not given in this way, either, except to the already abstract sense of sight: individual buildings are then "objects" only in photographs.)

It is important to recognize (or to admit) that this second series of questions or problems remains essentially phenomenological in its orientation: indeed, it is possible that the vice of our initial question lies there, that it still insists on posing the problem of the relationship of the individual subject and of the subject's "lived experience" to the architectural or urban spatial object, however the latter is to be construed. What is loosely called "structuralism" is now generally understood as the repudiation of this phenomenological "problematic" of such presuppostions as "experience": it has generated a whole new counterproblematic of its own, in which space — the individual building or the city itself — is taken as a text in which a whole range of "signs" and "codes" is combined, whether in the organic unity of a shared code, or in "collage" systems of various kinds, in structures of allusion to the past, or of ironic commentary on the present, or of radical disjunctures, in which some radically new sign (the Seagram Building or the Radiant City) *criticizes* the older sign system into which it dramatically erupts. Yet in another perspective it is precisely this last possibility that has been called back into question, and that can be seen as a replication, in more modern "structuralist" language, of our initial question. In all the arts, the new "textual" strategies stubbornly smuggled back into their new problematic the coordinates of the older political question, and of the older unexamined opposition between "authentic" and "inauthentic": for a time, the newer mediations produced seemingly new versions of the older (false?) problem, in the form of concepts of "subversion," the breaking of codes, their radical interruption or contestation (along with their predictable dialectical opposite, the notion of "co-optation"). It is the viability of these new solutions that is today generally in doubt: they now come to be felt as more utopianism, only of a negative or "critical" variety. They seemed at first to have repudiated the older positive and nostalgic ideals of a new utopian — authentic, non-alienated — space or art: yet their claim to punctual negativity — far more modest at first glance — now seems equally utopian in the bad sense. For even the project of criticizing, subverting, delegitimating, strategically interrupting, the established codes of a repressive social and spatial order has ultimately come to be understood as appealing to some conception of critical "self-consciousness," of critical distance, which today seems problematic; while on a more empirical level, it has been observed that the most subversive gesture itself hardens over into yet another form of being or positivity in its turn (just as the most negative *critical* stance loses its therapeutic and destructive shock value and slowly turns back into yet another critical ideology in its own right).

Is some third term beyond these two moments — the phenomenological and the structural — conceivable? Pierre Bourdieu, in his *Outline of a Theory of Practice*, explicitly attempts just such a dialectical move beyond these two "moments," both of which are for him indispensable, yet insufficient: the concept of "practice" — the social body's programming by its spatial text, now taken to be the "bottom line" both of everyday experience and of the legitimation of the social structure itself — while offered as just such a solution, has only been "tested" on the much simpler materials and problems of precapitalist space in the Kabyl village. Meanwhile, Henri Lefèbvre's conception of space as the fundamental category of politics and of the dialectic itself — the one great prophetic vision of these last years of discouragement and renunciation — has yet to be grasped in all its pathbreaking implications, let alone explored and implemented: although Lefèbvre's influential role as an ideologist and critic of French architecture today must be noted and meditated upon.

It is precisely a role of this kind that yet another logically possible position — faced with the dilemmas we have outlined above — explicitly repudiates: this is the position of Manfredo Tafuri, which in at least some of its more peremptory expressions has the merit of a stark and absolute simplicity. The position is stated most baldly in the note to the second Italian edition of *Theories and History of Architecture*: "one cannot 'anticipate' a class architecture (an architecture 'for a liberated society'); what is possible is the introduction of class criticism into architecture."[1] Although Tafuri's working judgments — in texts written over a number of years — are in fact far more nuanced and ambiguous than such a proposition might suggest, certain key elements can at once be isolated: 1) The architectural critic has no business being an "ideologist," that is, a visionary proponent of architectural styles of the future, "revolutionary" architecture, and the like: her role must be resolutely negative, the vigilant denunciation of existent or historical architectural ideologies. This position then tends to slip into a somewhat different one, namely that 2) the practicing architect, in *this* society and within the closure of capitalism as a system, cannot hope to devise a radically different, a revolutionary, or a "utopian" architecture or space either. 3) Without any conceivable normative conception of architectural space, of a space of radical difference from this one, the criticism

[1] Manfredo Tafuri, *Theories and History of Architecture*, trans. Giorgio Verrecchia (New York: Harper and Row, 1980), iii.

Precapitalist space: Kabyl village

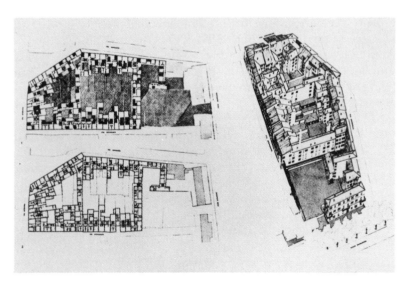

Commune of Bologna Technical Office, plan for the conservation of the historical center of Bologna, 1982

of buildings tends to be conflated with the criticism of the ideologies of such buildings; the history and criticism of architecture thus tends to fold back into the history and criticism of the various ideologies of architecture, the manifestos and the verbal expressions of the great architects themselves. 4) Political action is not renounced in such a position, or not *necessarily* (although more "pessimistic" readings of Tafuri are certainly possible). What is, however, affirmed here is consonant with the Althusserian tradition of the "semi-autonomy" of the levels and practices of social life: politics is radically disjoined from aesthetic (in this case, architectural) practice. The former is still possible, but only on *its* level, and architectural or aesthetic production can never be immediately political, it takes place somewhere else. Architects can therefore be political, like other individuals, but their architecture today cannot be political (a restatement of proposition 2, above). It follows, then, that 5) an architecture of the future will be concretely and practically possible only when the future has arrived, that is to say, after a total social revolution, a systemic transformation of this mode of production into something else.

This position, which inevitably has something of the fascination of uncompromising intransigence and of all absolutes, must be understood, as I shall try to show below in more detail, first of all within the history of contemporary Marxism, as a repudiation of what the Althusserians called Marxist "humanism" (including very specifically its "utopian" component as symbolically represented by Marcuse or by Lefèbvre himself). Its refusal to entertain the possibility of some properly Marxian "ideology" (which would seek to project alternate futures), its commitment to a resolutely critical and analytical Marxian "science" — by way of a restriction to the operation of denouncing the ideologies of the past and of a closed present — all these features betray some kinship with Adorno's late and desperate concept of a purely "negative dialectic." The ambiguity of such a position lies in its very instability, and the way in which it can imperceptibly pass over into a post-Marxism of the type endorsed by the French *nouveaux philosophes* or by Tafuri's collaborator, Massimo Cacciari. This is to suggest that Tafuri's position is *also* an ideology, and that one does not get out of ideology by refusing it or by committing oneself to negative and critical "ideological analysis."

Yet at this stage, such an evaluation remains at the level of mere opinion and in that form has little if any interest: in what follows I shall try to give it more content by examining Tafuri's work — and most notably his short, widely read, but dense and provocative *Architecture and Utopia*[2] —in three distinct perspectives. The first must be that of the Marxist context in which it was first produced, a context in which a series of significant but implicit moves may go unrecognized by the non-Marxist or American reader for want of the appropriate background. The second perspective (in no special order) will be that of the discursive form in which Tafuri works, namely historiography itself, and most particularly narrative history, whose formal dilemmas and problems today may be seen as determining (or at least over-determining) certain of Tafuri's organizing concepts. Finally, it will be appropriate to reconsider this considerable body of work (now largely available in English) in the context of a more vast, contemporary event, which has its own specifically American equivalents (and which is by no means limited to the field of architecture, although the battle lines have been drawn more dramatically there than in any other art) — namely the critique of high modernism, the increasingly omnipresent feeling that the modern movement itself is henceforth extinct: a feeling that has often been accompanied by the sense that we may therefore now be in something else, sometimes called postmodernism. It is, incidentally, a matter of no small significance, to which we shall return, that this second theme — the dawning of some new post-modernist moment or even "age" — is utterly alien to Tafuri himself and plays no role in his periodizing framework or in his historical narrative.

I want to deal first with the second of my three topics, namely that which has to do with historiography, with the problem of writing history, and in this case of writing the history of a discipline, an art, a medium. That there has been a crisis in narrative or storytelling history since the end of the nineteenth century is well known, as is the relationship between this crisis and that other crisis in the realistic novel itself: narrative history and the realistic novel are indeed closely related and in the greatest nineteenth-century texts virtually interchangeable. In our own time, this ongoing crisis has been re-thematized in terms of the critique of representation, one of the fundamental slogans of poststructuralism: briefly, the narrative representation of history necessarily tends to suggest that history is something you can see, be a witness to, be present at — an obviously inadmissible proposition. On the other hand, as the word itself suggests, history is always fundamentally storytelling, and must always be narrative in its very structure.

[2] Manfredo Tafuri, *Architecture and Utopia*, trans. Barbara Luigia La Penta (Cambridge: MIT Press, 1980).

This dilemma will not bother those for whom history-writing is not an essential task; if you are satisfied to do small-scale semiotic analyses of discrete or individual texts, or buildings, then presumably the problem of the writing of history, the telling of a historical story, will not unduly preoccupy you. I say "presumably" because I think that this problem also leaves its traces on such static analyses, and indeed it seems to be an empirical fact that the issues of history are returning everywhere today, not least within semiotics itself (the history of semiotics, the turn of semiotic analysis to the problem of genres, the problem of a semiotic of historical representation).

However, leaving other people to their concerns it will be clear that no issue is more central or more acute for those with some commitment to a dialectical tradition, since the dialectic has always for better or for worse been associated with some form or other of historical vision. For myself, I am much attracted by Louis Althusser's solution, which consists in proposing, in the midst of the crisis of historical representation and of narrative history, that the historian should conceive her task, not as that of producing a representation of history, but rather as that of producing the *concept* of history, a very different matter indeed.

But how is this to be done? Or rather, to be more modest about it, how has this actually been done in practice? From this perspective, it will be of interest to read *Architecture and Utopia* with a view toward determining the way in which it suggestively "produces the concept" of a dialectical history of architecture. But this is a rare enough achievement for one to want, initially, to juxtapose Tafuri's text with those very rare other realizations of this particular genre or form. I can think of only two contemporary dialectical histories of comparable intensity and intellectual energy: they are Adorno's *Philosophy of Modern Music* (a seminal text, on which Thomas Mann drew for his musical materials in *Doktor Faustus*) and, in the area of the history of literature, Roland Barthes's early and unequaled *Writing Degree Zero*. You will understand that this limited choice does not imply a lack of interest in the contributions that a Lukács, a Sartre, an Asor Rosa, or a Raymond Williams, among others, has made to the restructuring of traditional paradigms of literary history. What the three books I have mentioned have in common is not merely a new set of dialectical insights into literature, but the practice of a peculiar, condensed, allusive discursive form, a kind of textual *genre*, still exceedingly rare, which I shall call dialectical history.

Let me first single out a fundamental organizational feature which these three works share, and which I am tempted to see as the ultimate precondition to which they must painfully submit in order to practice dialectical thinking: this is the sense of Necessity, of necessary failure, of closure, of ultimate unresolvable contradictions and the impossibility of the future, which cannot have failed to oppress any reader of these texts, particularly readers who as practicing artists — whether architects, composers, or writers — come to them for suggestions and encouragement as to the possibility of future cultural production.

Adorno's discussion of musical history culminates, for instance, in Schoenberg's extraordinary "solution" — the twelve-tone system — which solves all of the dilemmas outstanding in previous musical history so completely as to make musical composition after Schoenberg superfluous (or at least regressive) from Adorno's perspective, yet which at the same time ends up as a baleful replication or mirror image of that very totalitarian socio-economic system from which it sought to escape in the first place. In Barthes's *Writing Degree Zero* the well-known ideal of "white writing" — far from being what it often looks like today, namely a rather complacent account of postmodernist trends — stood in its initial historical context and situation as an equally impossible solution to a dilemma that rendered all earlier practices of writing or style ideological and intolerable. Tafuri's account, finally, of the increasing closure of late capitalism (beginning in 1931, and intensifying dialectically after World War II), by systematically shutting off one aesthetic possibility after another, ends up conveying a paralyzing and asphyxiating sense of the futility of any architectural or urbanistic innovation on this side of that equally inconceivable watershed, a total social revolution.

It would be silly, or even worse, frivolous, to discuss these positions in terms of optimism or pessimism. Later on I shall have some remarks to make about the political presuppositions that account for (or at least overdetermine) some of Tafuri's attitudes here; what I prefer to stress now is the formal origin of these somber visions of the total system, which, far worse than Max Weber's iron cage, here descends upon human life and human creative praxis. The strengths of the readings and insights of Adorno, Barthes, and Tafuri in these works are for one thing inextricably bound up with their vision of history as an increasingly total or closed system. In other words, their ability to interpret a given work of art as a provisional "solution" is absolutely dependent on a perspective that reads the artwork against a context reconstructed or rewritten as a situation and a contradiction.

More than this, I find confirmation in these books for an

intuition I have expressed elsewhere, namely that the dialectic, or powerful dialectical history, must somehow always involve a vision of Necessity, or, if you prefer, must always tell the story of failure. "The owl of Minerva takes its flight at dusk": dialectical interpretation is always retrospective, always tells the necessity of an event, why it *had* to happen the way it did; and to do that, the event must already have happened, the story must already have come to an end. Yet as this will sound like an indictment of the dialectic (or as yet one more post-Marxist "proof" of its irre-cuperable Hegelian character), it is important to add that such histories of necessity and of determinate failure are equally inse-parable from some ultimate historical perspective of reconcilia-tion, of achieved socialism, of Marx's "end of prehistory."

The restructuring of the history of an art in terms of a series of situations, dilemmas, contradictions, in terms of which individual works, styles, and forms can be seen as so many responses or determinate symbolic acts: this is then a first key feature of dialectical historiography. But there is another no less essential one that springs to mind, at least when one thinks in terms of historical materialism, and that is the reversal associated with the term *materialism* itself, the anti-idealistic thrust, the rebuke and therapeutic humiliation of consciousness forced to reground itself in a painful awareness of what Marx called its "social determination." This second requirement is of course that which sets off the present texts sharply from old-fashioned Hegelian spiritual historiography, but which in turn threatens to undermine the historiographic project altogether, as in Marx's grim reminder in *The German Ideology*:

> We do not set out from what people say, imag-ine, or conceive, nor from people as narrated, thought of, imagined, conceived, in order to arrive at people in the flesh. We set out from real, active human beings, and on the basis of their real life-process we demonstrate the devel-opment of the ideological reflexes and echoes of this life-process. The phantoms formed in the human brain are also, necessarily, sublimates of their material life-process, which is empirically verifiable and bound to material premises. Mor-ality, religion, metaphysics, all the rest of ideol-ogy and their corresponding forms of conscious-ness, thus no longer retain their semblance of independence. They have no history, no devel-opment, in their own right; but it is rather human beings who, developing their material produc-

tion and relationships, alter, along with this, their real existence, their thinking, and the products of their thinking. Life is not determined by consciousness, but consciousness by life.[3]

Now the slogan of "materialism" has again become a very popular euphemism for Marxism: I have my own reasons for objecting to this particular ideological fashion on the left today: facile and dishonest as a kind of popular-front solution to the very real tensions between Marxism and feminism, the slogan also seems to me extraordinarily misleading as a synonym for "historical materialism" itself, since the very concept of "materialism" is a bourgeois Enlightenment (later positivist) concept, and fatally conveys the impression of a "determinism by the body" rather than, as in genuine dialectical Marxism, a "determination by the mode of production." At any rate, in the context that concerns us here — the description of "dialectical historiography" — the drawback of the word "materialism" is that it tends to suggest that only one form of dialectical reversal — the overthrow of idealism by materialism or a recall to matter — is at work in such books.

Actually, however, the dialectical shock, the reversal of our habits of idealism, can take many forms; and it is evident that in the dialectical history of an art its privileged targets will be the idealistic habits we have inherited in thinking about such matters and, in particular, Hegelian notions of the history of forms and styles, but also empiricist or structuralist notions of isolated texts. Still, it is best to see how these reversal-effects have been achieved in practice, rather than deducing them a priori in some dogmatic manner. And since none of these works ever raises one key issue of concern to everyone today, it is appropriate to preface a discussion of them with the indication of a fundamental form of contemporary "reversal" which may not leave them unscathed either: namely the way in which contemporary feminist critiques cut across the whole inherited system of the histories of art and culture by demonstrating the glaring absence from them, not merely of women as such, but, in the architectural area, of any consideration of the relationship between women's work and interior space, and between the domination of women and the city plan itself. For male intellectuals, this is the most stunning materialist reversal of all, since it calls *us* effectively into question at the same time that it disturbingly seems to discredit the very foundations and institutional presuppositions of the

[3] Karl Marx and Friedrich Engels, *The German Ideology* (New York: International, 1947), 14 – 15.

disciplines in question.

Indeed, the lesson for us in criticism of this kind may well be, among other things, that: that a materialist or dialectical historiography does its work ultimately by undermining the very foundations, framework, constitutive presuppositions, of the specialized disciplines themselves by unexpectedly demonstrating the existence, not necessarily of "matter" in that limited sense, but rather in general of an *Other* of the discipline, an outside, a limit, the revelation of the *extrinsic*, which it is felt to be scandalous and unscholarly to introduce into a carefully regulated traditional debate.

Adorno's book perhaps goes least far in this direction: the *Philosophy of Modern Music* operates its particular reversal by shifting from the subject (the great composers and their styles and works) to the object, the raw material, the tonal system itself, which as a peculiar "logic of content" has its own dynamics and generates fresh problems with every new solution, setting absolute limits to the freedom of the composer at every historical moment, its objective contradictions increasing in intensity and complexity with each of those new moments, until Schoenberg's "final solution" — the unification of vertical and horizontal, of harmony and counterpoint — seems to produce an absolute that is a full stop, beyond which composition cannot go: a success that is also, in genuine dialectical fashion, an absolute failure.

Barthes's reversal is useful in that his problematic (which is essentially that of the Sartre of *What Is Literature?*) is the most distant from the rhetoric of materialism and materiality and consists rather in a vision of the nightmare of history as blood guilt, and as that necessary and inevitable violence of the relationship of any group to the others which we call class struggle. Both writers — Sartre and Barthes — reverse our placid conceptions of literary history by demonstrating how every individual text, by its institutionalized signals, necessarily selects a particular readership for itself and thereby symbolically endorses the inevitable blood guilt of that particular group or class. Only whereas Sartre proposed the full utopian solution of a literature of praxis that would address itself to a classless society, Barthes ingeniously imagines a different way of escaping from the "nightmare of history," a kind of neutral or zero term, the projection of a kind of work from which all group or class signals have been eliminated: white or bleached writing, an escape from group blood guilt to the other side of group formation (which in later Barthes will be reoriented around reception rather than production and become the escape from class struggle into an equally non-individual kind of *jouissance* or punctual schizophrenic or perverse ecstasy, as in

The Pleasure of the Text).

    This is the moment to observe the temptation of the "zero degree" solution in Tafuri himself, where it constitutes one, but *only* one, of the provisional working possibilities very sparsely detectable in his pages. A Barthesian reading of Tafuri's account of Mies and the Seagram Building seems more plausible, as well as more historical, than a Heideggerian one, particularly if we attend to the content of Tafuri's proto-Mallarméan celebration of the glacial silence of this building, rather than to its rather Germanic language: "The 'almost nothing' has become a 'big glass' ... reflecting images of the urban chaos that surrounds the timeless Miesian purity.... It accepts [the shift and flux of phenomena], absorbs them to themselves in a perverse multi-duplication, like a Pop Art sculpture that obliges the American metropolis to look at itself reflected ... in the neutral mirror that breaks the city web. In this, architecture arrives at the ultimate limits of its own possibilities. Like the last notes sounded by the Doctor Faustus of Thomas Mann, alienation, having become absolute, testifies uniquely to its own presence, separating itself from the world to declare the world's incurable malady."[4] This is, however, less the endorsement of a Miesian aesthetic than a way of closing the historical narrative, and, as we shall see in a moment, of endowing the implacable and contradictory historical *situation* with an absolute power that such desperate non-solutions as Barthesian "bleached writing" or Miesian silence can only enhance.

    Returning for the moment to the strategies of the materialist reversal, Tafuri's use of such strategies is original in that it includes an apologia for the primacy of architecture over all the other arts (and thereby of architectural theory and criticism as well): but the apologia is distinctly untraditional and, one would think, not terribly reassuring for people professionally committed to this field of specialization. Architecture is for Tafuri supreme among the arts simply because its other or exterior is coeval with history and society itself, and it is susceptible therefore to the most fundamental materialist or dialectical reversal of all. To put it most dramatically, if the outer limit of the individual building is the material city itself, with its opacity, complexity, and resistance, then the outer limit of some expanded conception of the architectural vocation as including urbanism and city planning is the economic itself, or capitalism in the most overt and naked expression of its implacable power. So the great Central Euro-

---

[4] Manfredo Tafuri and Francesco Dal Co, *Modern Architecture* (New York: Abrams, 1979), 342.

Mies van der Rohe, Seagram Building, New York, 1954 – 1958

pean urbanistic projects of the 1920s (the *Siedlungen*, or workers' housing, in Berlin, Frankfurt, and Vienna) touch their other in the seemingly "extrinsic" obstacle of financial speculation and the rise in land and property values that causes their absolute failure and spells an end to their utopian vocation. But where for some traditional history of forms this is an extrinsic and somehow accidental, extraneous fact, which essentially has "nothing to do" with the purely formal values of these designs, in Tafuri's practice of the dialectic, this seemingly extrinsic situation is then drawn back into the dialectical spiral itself, and passes an absolute judgment of history proper upon such utopian forms.

These two dialectical reversals — the judgment on the project of an individual building, text, or "work of art" by the preexisting reality of the city itself; the subsequent judgment on aesthetics of urban planning and ensembles by that vaster "totality" which is capitalism itself — these are only two of the modes of reversal among many in Tafuri's little book: and it is this very richness of the forms of an anti-idealist turn, the dialectical suppleness of Tafuri's use of varied thematic oppositions, which makes his text both so fascinating and exemplary, and so bewilderingly dense and difficult to read. Other modes of reversal could be enumerated: most notably the unpleasant reminder of the professional status of intellectuals themselves and the ideological and idealistic distortions that result from that status; as well as the thematics of a Keynsian management of the "future" — a kind of credit and planning system of human life — which is one of the more novel subthemes of this work, and of its staging of the critique of modernist utopianism.

What must be stressed at this point, however, is the way in which the principal "event" of such dialectical histories — the contradiction itself, the fatal reversal of this or that aesthetic solution as it comes to grief against its own material underside — necessarily determines the form of their narrative closure and the kind of "ending" they are led to project. In all three, the present is ultimately projected as the final and most absolute contradiction, the "situation" which has become a blank wall, beyond which history cannot pass. Such an "end of history," or abolition of the future, is most open in Adorno, where it is paid for by the tragic "blind spot" of the philosopher-composer, who must on the one hand systematically reject the "other" of his culture (including the movement of popular or mass culture — contemptuously dismissed by Adorno under the all-purpose term "jazz" or "easy music," and that whole movement of Third World history and culture, which is the "repressed" of his Eurocentrism); on the other hand he must refuse even the development of advanced music beyond his "final stage," repudiating Stockhausen, electronic music, all of the developments of the fifties and sixties, with the same stubborn passion that leads him to bracket any conceivable *political* future in *Negative Dialectics*.

We have examined already the more ingenious conception of a "negative way" in Barthes's ideal of a zero degree of writing or in Tafuri's passing homage to Mies. What must now be underscored is the constitutive relationship between Tafuri's possibility of constructing dialectical history and his systematic refusal of what, in *Theories and History of Architecture*, is called "operative criticism"; that is, a criticism which, most strikingly in classical works like Giedion's *Space, Time and Architecture*, reads the past selectively and places an illusory historical analysis, the *appearance* of some "objective" historical narrative, in the service of what is in reality an architectural *manifesto*, the "normative" projection of some new style, the *project* of future work and future possibilities: "the planning of a precise poetical tendency, anticipated in its structures and derived from historical analyses programmatically distorted and finalized";[5] — in short, "ideological criticism [that] substitutes ready-made judgments of value (prepared for immediate use) for analytical rigor."[6] But this judgment on the spurious appropriation of the past in the service of an endorsement of aesthetic action in the present implies that "rigorous" analytical history must in turn be bought by a stoic renunciation of action and of value, and a well-nigh Hegelian renunciation of all possible futures, in order that the owl of Minerva be able to wing its flight into the past. Tafuri's "pessimism" is thus to be seen as a formal necessity of the generic structure of his text — dialectical historiography — rather than an "opinion" or a "position" in its own right.

Unfortunately, one also cannot help but read it as just such an opinion or position; and at this point a purely formal and textual necessity intersects with and is overdetermined by ideology, and becomes the vehicle for a whole set of ideological messages and signals that has real content and that can best be appreciated by way of the Marxian traditions from which it emerges.

It seems to me most convenient to decode these signals in the context of a current and general left appropriation of the older right-wing "end of ideology" slogans of the late 1950s. In the period of the Eisenhower era and the great American celebration, the "end of ideology" meant not merely the death of Marxism,

---

[5] *Theories and History*, 141.
[6] Ibid., 153.

but also the good news of the end of the classical capitalism ana-
tomized by Marx, and the apparition of some new social order
whose dynamics were no longer based on production and associated with social classes and their struggle, but rather on a new
principle, which was therefore to be seen as in all those senses
"beyond ideology." This new social system would then be
named, by the ex-Marxist right-wing theorists of an "end of
ideology," most notably Daniel Bell, "post-industrial society"[7]
(others would call it consumer society, media society, consumer
capitalism, and so forth); and its dynamic would be characterized
by the primacy of knowledge, of scientific and technological
know-how, and of a new social group (no longer a class in the
Marxian sense), namely the technocrats.

For obvious reasons, the left repudiated this kind of
analysis for a number of years, remaining intent on demonstrating that the classical analyses and concepts of Marx's *Capital* were
still valid for the period that Bell and others were intent on
describing as the dialectical mutation of "post-industrial society."
It is clear that something of the force of Bell's theory derived from
the optimism of the Eisenhower era, the period of American
empire, and a global *pax americana*; and that history itself, better
than any left countertheories or critiques, undertakes to pro-
nounce judgment on the "end of ideology," "post-industrial
society" thesis and to lay it to rest in our own moment of the
return of more classical global economic crisis, worldwide
depression, unemployment, and the like.

Paradoxically, however, it was precisely in the interven-
ing years that the left itself caught up with the thesis of a new
historical moment, a radical historical break, and produced its
own version of the "end of ideology" thesis. This had something
to do with changes in social atmosphere and temperature, and
with the alteration of the quality of life in the advanced world;
that is to say, with mutations in the appearance or surface of
social life. It became clear to everyone, in other words, that with
consumerism, with the enormous penetration and colonization of
the apparatus of the media, with the release of new non-class
social forces in the sixties — forces associated with race and gen-
der, with nationalism and religion, with marginality (as in the
case of students or the permanently unemployed) — something
decisive had changed in the very "reality of the appearance" of
capitalism. What the new Marxian version of this would do was

---

[7] See his two books, *The Coming of Post-Industrial Society: A Venture in Social Fore-
casting* (New York: Basic Books, 1973), and *The Cultural Contradictions of Capitalism*
(New York: Basic Books, 1976).

to explain the originality of the features of so-called post-industrial society as a new stage of capitalism proper, in which the old contradictions of capital were still at work, but in unexpectedly new forms. The features enumerated by people like Bell — for example, the primacy of science, the role of bureaucracy, and so forth — would be retained, but interpreted very differently in the light of a new moment that can be called "late capitalism" or the multinational world system (in the traditional Marxian periodization this would be a third moment of capitalism, after those of classical market capitalism and of imperialism and monopoly, and could be dated from the immediate postwar period in the United States and the late 1950s in Europe).[8] I do not have time to go into this extremely important new Marxian theory of the contemporary world, but must, before returning to Tafuri, underscore two of its significant features.

First, it is the theory of something like a total system, marked by a global deployment of capital around the world (even, on many accounts, reaching into the still far from autonomous economic dynamics of the nascent socialist countries), and effectively destroying the older coherence of the various national situations. The total system is marked also by the dynamism with which it now penetrates and colonizes the two last surviving enclaves of Nature within the older capitalism: the unconscious and the precapitalist agriculture of the Third World — the latter is now systematically undermined and reorganized by the Green Revolution, while the former is effectively mastered by what the Frankfurt School used to call the "culture industry," that is, the media, mass culture, and the various other techniques of the commodification of the mind. I should also add that this new quantum leap of capital now menaces that other precapitalist enclave within older capitalism, namely the non-paid labor of the older interior or home or family, thereby in contradictory fashion unbinding and liberating that enormous new social force of women, who immediately then pose an uncomfortable new threat to the new social order.

On the other hand, if the new expansion of multinational or late capitalism at once triggers various new forms of struggle and resistance, as in the great revolts of the 1960s, it also tends to be accompanied by the mood of pessimism and hopelessness that must naturally enough accompany the sense of a total system, with nothing outside itself, within which now local revolts and

[8] The most systematic and powerful exposition of this theory is found in Ernest Mandel, *Late Capitalism* (London: New Left Books, 1975), on which I draw heavily here.

resistances come to be seen, not as the emergence of new forces and a new logic of a radically different future, but rather mere inversions within the system, punctual reversals of this or that systemic feature: no longer dialectical in their force, but merely structural(-ist). The Marxist response to this increasing windless closure of the system will be varied: it can take the form of a substitution of the time-scale of the prognosis of the *Grundrisse* for that, far more imminent, of Capital proper.[9] In the *Grundrisse*, indeed, Marx seems to project a far greater resiliency for capitalism than in *Capital* itself, one which better accommodates the unexpected new vitality and dynamism of the system after World War II. The key feature of this position will be the insistence on what is, after all, a classical notion of Marx, namely that a socialist revolution and a socialist society are not possible until capitalism has somehow exhausted all its possibilities, but also not until capitalism has become a worldwide and global fact, in which universal commodification is combined with a global proletarianization of the work force, a transformation of all humanity (including the peasants of the Third World) into wage workers. In that case, the chances for socialism are relegated into some far future, while the ominous nature of the current "total system" becomes rather positive again, since it marks precisely the quantum progression toward that final global state. But this means, in addition, that not only can there not be socialism in one country, there cannot be anything like socialism in one block of countries: socialist revolution here is by definition global revolution or it is nothing. And equally obviously, there can be no emergence of a different social system within the interstices of the old, within this or that sector of capitalism proper. Here, I think, you will have already recognized the perspective that is characteristic of Tafuri's work: there can be no qualitative change in any element of the older capitalist system — as, for instance, in architecture or urbanism — without beforehand a total revolutionary and systemic transformation. (Total systems theory can, of course, also be explained in terms of the kind of textual determinism already evoked above: the purpose of the theorist is to build as powerful a model of capital as possible, and as all-embracing, systemic, seamless, and self-perpetuating. Thus, if the theorist succeeds, he fails; since the more powerful the model constructed, the less possibility will be foreseen in it for any form of human resistance, any chance of structural transformation.)

Yet the meaning of this stark and absolute position, this

---

[9] See Martin Nicolaus, "The Unknown Marx," in Klare and Howard, *The Hidden Dimension*.

diagnosis of the total system of late or multinational capital, cannot be grasped fully without taking into account the alternative position of which it is the symbolic repudiation: and this is what may be called neo-Gramscianism, the more "optimistic" assessment of some possible "long march through the institutions," which counterposes a new conception of some gradualist "war of position" for the classical Leninist model of the "war of maneuver," the all-or-nothing seizure of power. There are, of course, many reasons why radical Italian intellectuals today should have become fatigued with the Gramscian vision, paradoxically at the very moment in which it has come to seem reinvigorating for the left in other national situations in Europe and elsewhere: most obvious of these reasons is the thirty-year institutionalization of Gramsci's thought within the Italian Communist Party (and the assimilation of Gramsci, in the Italian context, to that classical form of dialectical thought which is everywhere systematically repudiated by a Nietzschean post-Marxism). Nor should we forget to underscore the structural ambiguity or polysemousness of the basic Gramscian texts, which, written in a coded language beneath the eyes of the Fascist censor, can either be "translated back" into classical Leninism, or on the contrary read as a novel *inflection* of Leninism in a new direction, as a post-Leninism or stimulating new form of *neo*-Marxism. There are therefore "objectively" many distinct Gramscis, between which it would be frivolous to attempt to decide which is the "true" one. I want, however, to suggest that with some Gramscian alternative, the possibility of a very different perspective on architecture and urbanism today is also given: so that the implications of this further digression are not a matter of Marxist scholastics, nor are they limited to purely political consequences.

At least two plausible yet distinct readings of the Gramscian slogan, the struggle for "hegemony," must be proposed at this point. What is at stake is the meaning of that "counterhegemony" which oppositional forces are called upon to construct within the ongoing dominance of the "hegemony" of capital: and the interpretive dilemma here turns on the (false) problem of a materialist or an idealist reading. If the Gramscian struggle, in other words, aims essentially at the *preparation* of the working class for some eventual seizure of power, then "counterhegemony" is to be understood in purely superstructural terms, as the elaboration of a set of ideas, countervalues, cultural styles, that are virtual or *anticipatory*, in the sense that they "correspond" to a material, institutional base that has not yet "in reality" been secured by political revolution itself.

The temptation is therefore to argue for a "materialist"

reading of Gramsci on the basis of certain key figures or tropes in the classical Marxian texts. One recalls, for example, the "organic" formulations of the 1859 Preface to the *Critique of Political Economy*: "New, higher relations of production never appear before the material conditions of their existence have matured within the womb of the old society ... productive forces developing in the womb of bourgeois society create the material conditions for the solution of the antagonism [of all previous history as class conflict]."[10] There must also be noted the celebrated figure with which, in passing, the Marx of *Capital* characterizes the status of "commerce" within the quite different logic of the "ancient" mode of production: "existing in the interstices of the ancient world, like the gods of Epicurus in the *intermundia* or the Jews in the pores of Polish society."[11]

Such figures suggest something like an *enclave* theory of social transition, according to which the emergent future, the new and still nascent social relations that announce a mode of production that will ultimately displace and subsume the as yet still dominant one, is theorized in terms of small yet strategic pockets or beachheads within the older system. The essentially *spatial* nature of the characterization is no accident and conveys something like a historical tension between two radically different types of space, in which the emergent yet more powerful kind will gradually extend its influence and dynamism over the older form, fanning out from its initial implantations and gradually "colonizing" what persists around it. Nor is this a mere poetic vision: the political realities that have been taken as the "verification" and the concrete embodiment of "enclave theory" in contemporary society are the legendary "red communes" of Italy today, most notably Bologna, whose administration by the Communist Party has seemed to demarcate them radically from the corruption and inefficiency of the capitalist nation-state within which, like so many foreign bodies, they are embedded. Tafuri's assessment of such communes is particularly instructive:

> The debate over the historical centers and the experience of Bologna have shown that architectural and urbanistic proposals cannot be put to the test outside definite political situations, and then only within improved public structures for control. This has effected a substantial modification in the role of the architectural profession,

[10] Karl Marx, *Contribution to a Critique of Political Economy* (New York: International, 1970), 21.
[11] Karl Marx, *Capital*, vol.I (London: Penguin, 1976), 172.

even further redimensioned and characterized by an increasing change in the traditional forms of patronage and commissioning…. Although what [the new left city administrations] have inherited is in a desperate state and the financial difficulties are staggering, one can hope that from this new situation may come the realization of the reforms sought for decades. It is on this terrain that the Italian workers' movements are summoned to a historical test, whose repercussions may prove to be enormous, even outside Italy.[12]

These lines (written, to be sure, in the more favorable atmosphere of 1976) betray a rather different Tafuri than the somber historiographer of some "end of history" who predominates in the preceding pages.

What complicates this picture, however, is the discovery that it is precisely some such "enclave theory" that in Tafuri's analysis constitutes the utopianism of the modern movement in architecture; that, in other words, Tafuri's critique of the International Style, the informing center of all his works, is first and foremost a critique of the latter's enclave theory itself. Le Corbusier, for example, spoke of avoiding political revolutions, not because he was not committed to "revolution," but rather because he saw the construction and the constitution of new space as the most revolutionary act, and one that could "replace" the narrowly political revolution of the mere seizure of power (and if the experience of a new space is associated with a whole transformation of everyday life itself, Le Corbusier's seemingly antipolitical stance can be reread as an *enlargement* of the very conception of the political, and as having anticipatory kinship with conceptions of "cultural revolution," which are far more congenial to the spirit of the contemporary left). Still, the demiurgic hubris of high modernism is fatefully dramatized by such visions of the towers of the Plan Voisin, which stride across a fallen landscape like H. G. Wells's triumphant Martians, or of the gigantic symbolic structures of the Unités d'habitation, the Algiers plan, or Chandigarh, which are apocalyptically to sound the knell of the cramped and insalubrious hovels that lie dwarfed beneath their prophetic shadow. We shall enter shortly into the terms of Tafuri's critique of modernism itself: suffice it to say for the moment that its cardinal sin is precisely to identify (or conflate) the political and the aesthetic, and to foresee a political and

---

[12] *Modern Architecture*, 322.

social transformation that is henceforth at one with the formal processes of architectural production itself. All of which is easier to demonstrate on the level of empirical history, where the new enclaves of the International Style manifestly failed to regenerate anything around them; or where, when they did have the dynamic and radiating influence predicted for them by the masters, the results, if anything, were even more depressing, generating a whole series of dismal glass boxes in their own image, or a multiplication of pseudo-Corbusian towers in the desolation of parks that have become the battleground of an unending daily war of race and class. Even the great emblem of the "red communes" can from this perspective be read differently: for it can equally well be argued that they are not enclaves at all — not laboratories in which original social relations of the future are being worked out, but rather simply the administration of inherited capitalist relations, albeit conducted in a different spirit of social commitment than that of the Christian Democrats.

This uninspiring balance sheet would settle the fate of the Gramscian alternative, were the "enclave theory" its only plausible interpretation. The latter, however, may be seen as an overly reductive and rather defensively "materialist" conception of the politics of space; but it can equally well be argued that Gramsci's notion of hegemony (along with the later and related idea of cultural revolution) rather attempts to displace the whole distinction of materialism versus idealism (and along with it, of the traditional concept of base and superstructure). It will therefore no longer be "idealist" in the bad, old sense to suggest that counter-hegemony means producing and keeping alive a certain alternate "idea" of space, of urban, daily life, and the like. It would then no longer be so immediately significant (or so practically and historically crippling) that architects in the West do not — owing to the private property system — have the opportunity to project and construct collective ensembles that express and articulate original social relations (and needs and demands) of a collective type: the essential would rather be that they are able to form conceptions and utopian images of such projects, against which to develop a self-consciousness of their concrete activities in this society (it being understood, in Tafuri's spirit, that such collective projects would only practically and materially be possible after a systemic transformation of society). But such utopian ideas are as objective as material buildings: their possibilities — the possibility of conceiving such new space — have conditions of possibility as rigorous as any material artifact. Those conditions of possibility are to be found, first and foremost, in the uneven development of world history, and in the existence, elsewhere, in the Second and

Third Worlds, of projects and constructions that are not possible in the First: this concrete existence of radically different spaces elsewhere (of whatever unequal realization) is what objectively opens the possibility for the coming into being and development of "counterhegemonic values" here. A role is thereby secured for a more "positive" and Gramscian architectural criticism, over against Tafuri's stubbornly (and therapeutically) negative variety, his critical refusal of utopian speculation on what is not possible within the closure of the multinational system. In reality, both of these critical strategies are productive alternately according to the situation itself, and the public to which the ideological critic must address herself; and there is no particular reason to lay down either of these useful weapons. It is at any rate worth quoting yet another appreciation of Tafuri — this one, unexpectedly, of the Stalinallee — in order to show that his practical criticism is often a good deal more ambivalent than his theoretical slogans (and also further to dispel the feeling that the celebration of Mies's negative mysticism, quoted above, amounts to anything like a definitive position):

> However, in the case [of the Stalinallee, in East Berlin] it would be wrong to regard what resulted as purely ideological or propagandistic; in reality, the Stalinallee is the fulcrum of a project of urban reorganization affecting an entire district, establishing an axis of development toward the Tiergarten different from that developed historically. In addition, this plan inverts the logical manner in which a bourgeois city expands by introducing into the heart of the metropolis the residence as a decisive factor. The monumental bombast of the Stalinallee — now renamed Karl Marx Allee — was conceived to put in a heroic light an urbanistic project that set out to be different. In fact, it succeeds perfectly in expressing the presupposition for the construction of the new socialist city, which rejects divisions between architecture and urbanism and aspires to impose itself as a unitary structure.[13]

Such a text can evidently be used to support either position: the negative one, that such a collective project, with its transcendence of the opposition building/city, is only possible *after* a revolutionary transformation of social relations as a whole; or the

---

[13] *Modern Architecture*, 322, 326.

Madelon Vriesendorp, "The City of the Captive Globe," from Delirious New York, *1978*

more Gramscian one outlined above, that the very existence of such an ensemble in some other space of the world creates a new force field that cannot but have its influence even over those architects for whom such a project is scarcely a "realistic" possibility.

Still, until now we have not considered what kind of "total system" it is that sets limits to the practical transformation of space in our time; nor have we drawn the other obvious consequence from the Marxian theorization of "consumer society" or of the new moment of late capitalism, namely, that to such a new moment there very well may correspond a new type of culture or cultural dynamic. This is therefore the time to introduce our third theme or problem, namely that of postmodernism and of the critique of classical or high modernism itself. For the economic periodization of capital into three rather than two stages (that of "late" or multinational capitalism being now added to the more traditional moments of "classical" capitalism and of the "monopoly stage" or "state of imperialism") suggests the possibility of a new periodization on the level of culture as well: from this perspective, the moment of "high" modernism, of the International Style, and of the classical modern movement in all the arts — with their great *auteurs* and their utopian monuments, Mallarméan "Books of the World," fully as much as Corbusian Radiant Cities — would "correspond" to that second stage of monopoly and imperialist capitalism that came to an end with the Second World War. Its "critique" therefore coincides with its extinction, its passing into history, as well as with the emergence, in the third stage of "consumer capital," of some properly postmodernist practice of pastiche, of a new free play of styles and historicist allusions now willing to "learn from Las Vegas," a moment of surface rather than of depth, of the "death" of the old individual subject or bourgeois ego, and of the schizophrenic celebration of the commodity fetishism of the image, of a now "delirious New York" and a countercultural California, a moment in which the logic of media capitalism penetrates the logic of advanced cultural production itself and transforms the latter to the point where such distinctions as those between high and mass culture lose their significance (and where the older notions of a "critical" or "negative" value of advanced or modernist art may also no longer be appropriate or operative).

As I have observed, Tafuri refuses this periodization, and we shall observe him positioning his critique of the postmoderns beneath the general category of a still high modernist utopianism, of which they are seen merely as so many epigones. Still, in this country and for this public, the thrust of his critique of utopian architecture will inevitably be associated with the generalized reaction here against the older hegemonic values and norms of the International Style, about which we must attempt to take an ambivalent and nuanced position. It is certain, for instance — as books like Tom Wolfe's recent *From Bauhaus to Our House* readily testify — that the critique of high modernism can spring from reactionary and "philistine" impulses (in both the aesthetic and the political sense) and can be belatedly nourished by all the old middle-class resistances that the modern movement met and aroused while it was still fresh. Nor does it seem implausible that in certain national situations, most notably in those of the former fascist countries, the antimodernist position is still essentially and unambiguously at one, as Habermas has suggested,[14] with political reaction: if so, this would explain Tafuri's decision to uncouple a reasoned critique of modernism from the adoption or exposition of any more "positive" aesthetic ideology. In the United States, however, whatever the ultimate wisdom of applying a similar strategy, the cultural pull and attractiveness of the concept of postmodernism clearly complicates the situation in ways that need to be clarified.

It will therefore be useful to retrace our steps for the moment and, however briefly, to work through the terms of Tafuri's critique of modernism as he outlines it for us in *Architecture and Utopia*, where we meet a left-wing version of the "end of ideology" roughly consistent with the periodizations of some new stage of capital that have just been evoked. In this view, ideas as such — ideology in the more formal sense of a whole system of legitimizing beliefs — are no longer significant elements in the social reproduction of late capitalism, something that was obviously not the case in its earlier stages. Thus the great bourgeois revolutionary ideology of "liberty, equality, and fraternity" was supremely important in securing the universal consent of a variety of social classes to the new political and economic order: this ideology was thus also, in Tafuri's use of the term, a utopia, or rather, its ideologizing and legitimizing function was concealed behind a universalizing and utopian rhetoric. In the late nineteenth century — particularly in the French Third Republic (the "Republic of the Professors") — positivism, with its militant anticlericalism and its ideal of a lay or secular education, suggests the degree to which official philosophy was still felt to be a crucial terrain of ideological struggle and a supreme weapon

[14] See Jürgen Habermas, "Modernity versus Postmodernity," in *New German Critique*, no.22 (winter 1981), 3-18. (The whole issue, which centers on a discussion of Habermas's theses, is of great interest.)

for securing the unity of the state; while in our own time, until recently, what is generally called New Deal liberalism (or in Europe, the social democracy of the welfare states) performed an analogous function.

It is all this that would seem to be in question today. We shall want, Adorno says somewhere, to take into account the possibility that in our time the commodity is its own ideology: the practices of consumption and consumerism, on that view, themselves are then enough to reproduce and legitimate the system, no matter what "ideology" you happen to be committed to. In that case, not abstract ideas, beliefs, ideologies, or philosophical systems, but rather the immanent practices of daily life now occupy the functional position of "ideology" in its other larger systemic sense. And if so, this development can serve clearly as one explanation for the waning power of the utopian ideologies of high modernism as well. Indeed, Tafuri explicitly associates the demiurgic value of architectural planning in the modern masters with the Keynesian ideal of the control of the *future*. In both versions, utopia is the dream of "a 'rational' domination of the future, the elimination of the *risk* it brings with it":[15] "Even for Le Corbusier the absolute of form is the complete realization of a constant victory over the uncertainty of the future."[16] It is therefore logical enough that both these ultimate middle-class ideologies or utopias should disappear together, and that their concrete "critique" should be less a matter of intellectual self-consciousness, than simply a working out of history itself.

But "ideology" has a somewhat different focus in Tafuri's schematic overview of bourgeois architectural thinking, from the dissolution of the baroque to our own time, where these varied aesthetic utopias are analyzed in terms of something closer to a Hegelian "ruse of reason" or of history itself. Their utopian form thus proves to be an instrument in the edification of a business system and the new dynamism of capital. Whatever content they claimed in themselves, their concrete effects, their more fundamental function, lay in the systematic destruction of the past. Thus the emergence of secular conceptions of the city in the eighteenth century is first and foremost to be read as a way of clearing away the older culture: "The deliberate abstraction of Enlightenment theories of the city served ... to destroy baroque schemes of city planning and development."[17] In much the same way, the dawn of modernism proper — the moment in which ideology is overtly transformed into utopia, in which "ideology

[15] *Architecture and Utopia*, 52.
[16] Ibid., 129.

77

had to negate itself as such, break its own crystallized forms and throw itself entirely into the "construction of the future,"[18] this supreme moment of Freud and Nietzsche, of Weber and Simmel, and of the birth of high modernism in all the arts — was in reality for Tafuri a purely destructive operation in which residual ideologies and archaic social forms were systematically dissolved. The new utopianism of high modernism thus unwittingly and against the very spirit of its revolutionary and utopian affirmations prepared the terrain for the omnipotence of the fully "rationalized" technocratic plan, for the universal planification of what was to become the total system of multinational capital: "The unmasking of the idols that obstructed the way to a global rationalization of the productive universe and its social dominion became the new historical task of the intellectual."[19] It also became the historic mission of the various cultural avant-gardes themselves, for which, in reality, although not according to their own manifestos, "the autonomy of formal construction" as its deepest practical function has "to plan the disappearance of the subject, to cancel the anguish caused by the pathetic (or ridiculous) resistance of the individual to the structures of domination that close in upon him or her."[20] Therefore whatever avant-garde or architectural aesthetic utopias thought they were intent on achieving, in the real world of capital and in their effective practice, those ends are dialectically reversed, and serve essentially to reinforce the technocratic total control of the new system of the bureaucratic society of planned consumption.

We may now return to the beginnings of Tafuri's story in the eighteenth century. The Enlightenment attempt to think of urbanism in some new and more fully rational way generates two irreconcilable alternatives: one path is that of architecture as the "instrument of social equilibrium," the "geometric silence of Durand's formally codified building types," "the uniformity ensured by preconstituted formal systems."[21] The other is that of a "science of sensations,"[22] a kind of "excessive symbolism"[23] which we may interpret as the conception of a libidinal resistance within the system, the breakthrough of desire into the grids of power and control. These two great utopian anitheses, Saint-Simon versus Fourier, if you like, or Lenin versus Marcuse, are

---

[17] *Architecture and Utopia*, 8.
[18] Ibid., 50.
[19] Ibid., 51.
[20] *Architecture and Utopia*, 73.
[21] Ibid., 13.
[22] Ibid., 11.
[23] Ibid., 13.

Plan of Karlsruhe, mid-eighteenth century

Plan of Washington, D.C., 1800, based on Pierre Charles L'Enfant's plan of 1791

then for Tafuri the ideological double-bind of a thinking imprisoned in capitalist relations. They are at once then unmasked in Piranesi's contemporary and nightmarish synthesis of the Campo Marzio, and also, unexpectedly, given a longer lease on life in the New World, where, in the absence of feudalism and in the presence of the open frontier, the new urban synthesis of Washington, D.C., will have a vitality that European efforts are forbidden.

Interestingly enough, in our present context, these two alternatives also correspond roughly to the analyses of Adorno and Barthes respectively. The first utopian alternative, that of rationalization, will little by little formulate its program in terms of overcoming the opposition between whole and part, between urban plan and individual architectural monument, between the molar and the molecular, between the "urban organism as a whole" and the "elementary cell" or building blocks of the individual building (Hilberseimer). But it is precisely this "unified field theory" of the macro- and the micro- toward which the work of a Corbusier strives, which is projected, in Adorno's book, by Schoenberg's twelve-tone system, the ultimate abolition of the gap between counterpoint and harmony, between overall form and the dynamics of the individual musical "parole" or theme. But Schoenberg's extraordinary synthesis is sterile, and in architecture the "unified field theory" destroys the individual work or building as such: "The single building is no longer an 'object'; it is only the place in which the elementary assemblage of single cells assumes physical form; since these cells are elements reproducible *ad infinitum*, they conceptually embody the prime structures of a production line that excludes the old concepts of 'place' or "space."[24] This utopian impulse has then ended up rationalizing the object world more extensively and ferociously than anything Ford or Taylor might have done on his own momentum.

Yet the second, or libidinal, strategy is no less "ideological" in its ultimate results: Barthes's intellectual trajectory is a complicated one, and I will not take the time here to insert him neatly back into this scheme (although I think something like this could be done). Suffice it to observe that, following Benjamin, Tafuri sees this second libidinal strategy in its emergence in Baudelaire as having unexpected subjective consequences that harmonize with the objective external planification achieved above: "Baudelaire had discovered that the commercialization of the poetic product can be accentuated by the poet's very attempt to free himself from his objective conditions."[25] The new vanguard subjectivity, in other words, ends up training the

---

[24] *Architecture and Utopia*, 105.

consumer for life in the industrial city, teaching "the ideology of the correct use of the city,"[26] freeing the aesthetic consumer from "objects that were offered to judgment" and substituting "a process to be lived and used as such."[27] This particular strategy now prolongs itself into, revitalizes itself in the postmodernist ideologies and aesthetics of the present period, denounced by Tafuri in a memorable page:

> Thus the city is considered in terms of a suprastructure. Indeed art is now called upon to give the city a suprastructural guise. Pop art, op art, analysis of the urban "imageability," and the "prospective aesthetic" converge in this objective. The contradictions of the contemporary city are resolved in multivalent images, and by figuratively exalting that formal complexity they are dissimulated. If read with adequate standards of judgment this formal complexity is nothing other than the explosion of the irremediable dissonances that escape the plan of advanced capital. The recovery of the concept of art thus serves this new cover-up role. It is true that whereas industrial design takes a lead position in technological production and conditions its quality in view of an increase in consumption, pop art, reutilizing the residues and castoffs of that production, takes its place in the rear guard. But this is the exact reflection of the twofold request now made to the techniques of visual communication. Art which refuses to take its place in the vanguard of the production cycle actually demonstrates that the process of consumption tends to the infinite. Indeed even the rejects, sublimated into useless or nihilist objects which bear a new *value of use*, enter into the production-consumption cycle, if only through the back door. This art that deliberately places itself in the rear guard is also indicative of the refusal to come to terms with the contradictions of the city and resolve them completely; to transform the city into a totally organized machine without useless squanderings of an archaic character or generalized dysfunction. In

[25] Ibid., 92.
[26] *Architecture and Utopia*, 84.
[27] *Architecture and Utopia*, 101.

this phase it is necessary to persuade the public that the contradiction, imbalances, and chaos typical of the contemporary city are inevitable. Indeed the public must be convinced that this chaos contains an *unexplored richness*, unlimited utilizable possibilities, and qualities of the "game" now made into new fetishes for society.

The power of such negative critiques of ideology (which construe ideology exclusively in terms of "false consciousness") lies in the assumption that everything that does not effectively disrupt the social reproduction of the system may be considered as part and parcel of the reproduction of that system. The anxieties provoked in almost everyone by such an implacable and absolute position are probably healthy and therapeutic in one way or another. As I have begun to suggest before, however, the real problem in such an analysis lies elsewhere, in the assumption that "social reproduction" in late capitalism takes much the same form as in the earlier period of high modernism, and that what some of us call the "postmoderns" simply replicate the old modernist solutions at lower levels of intensity and originality. Thus Philip Johnson's "ambiguous eclecticism ends up as mere jugglery";[29] "the works of Louis Kahn and the British architect James Stirling represent two opposite attempts to breathe life into a seemingly moribund art";[30] Robert Venturi's *Complexity and Contradiction in Architecture* flattens out the New Critical concepts of ambiguity and contradiction, dehistoricizing them and emptying them of all their tragic (and properly high modernist) tension, with a view toward "justifying personal planning choices rather more equivocal than ambiguous."[31]

Yet there would seem to be a certain inconsistency in the reproach that the newer architects fail to achieve even that tragic tension that was itself considered to be utopian and ideological in the masters. The other face of this inconsistency can then be detected in the consonance and profound historical kinship between Tafuri's analysis of modernism and the onslaughts of the postmodernists, most notably Venturi himself, a critique that goes well beyond the usual themes of the hubris of central planning,[32] the single-function conception of space, and the puritanism of the streamlining abhorrence of ornament. Venturi's analysis, particularly in *Learning from Las Vegas*, centers specifically on

---

[28] *Architecture and Utopia*, 137,139.
[29] *Modern Architecture*, 397.
[30] Ibid., 400.
[31] *Theories and History*, 213.

the dialectic (and the contradiction) between the building and the city, between architecture and urbanism, which also forms one of the major strands in the historiography of the Italian theorist. The monumental duck of the International Style, it will be recalled — like Mallarmé's *Livre*, like Bayreuth, like *Finnegans Wake* or Kandinsky's mystical painting — proposes itself, as we have already suggested, as a radically different, revolutionary, or subversive enclave from which little by little the whole surrounding fabric of fallen social relations is to be regenerated and transformed. Yet in order to stage itself as a *foyer* of this kind, the "duck" must first radically separate itself from that environment in which it stands: it thereby comes slowly, by virtue of that very inaugural disjunction, that constitutive self-definition and isolation, to be not a building but a *sculpture*: after the fashion of Barthes's concept of connotation, it ends up — far from emitting a message with a radically new content — simply designating itself and signifying itself, celebrating its own disconnection as a message in its own right.

Whatever else may be said about the architecture of postmodernism — and however it is to be judged politically and historically — it seems important to recognize that it does not seek to do *that* but rather something very different. It may no longer embody the utopian ideology of high modernism, may indeed in that sense be vacuous of any utopian or protopolitical

---

[32] The critique of central planning, as in Peter Blake, as powerful and persuasive as it is, seems to me extremely ambiguous for the following reason. A perfectly correct and well-documented thesis of this kind can *also* be the occasion for the production of, or investment by, a whole ideology or metaphysics: most notably in the binary opposition between intention or plan and tradition or organic growth. (This ideology is already present in Christopher Alexander's "A City Is Not a Tree," but its full-blown transformation into a metaphysic can most dramatically be observed in Deleuze and Guattari's "Rhizome" (in *Mille Plateaux*). In this form, of course, it recapitulates the oldest counterrevolutionary position of all, that of Edmund Burke in the *Réflexions on the French Revolution*, where Jacobin hubris is counterposed against the slow and organic growth of social life. On the political level, the left traditions include a number of counterpositions that work against the emergence of such a stark and ideological opposition: most notably in concepts of federation and the "withering away of the state" (the Paris Commune), of *autogestion* or workers' self-management, and of council communism. But in the area of architecture or urbanism it is rather hard to see what form such counterpositions might take: least persuasive, to my mind, is the idea that people will rebuild their own dwellings as they go along (see for example Philippe Boudon, *Lived-In Architecture* [Cambridge: MIT Press, 1972], where the idea that Le Corbusier would have approved of all this, let alone intended it to happen that way, seems most disingenuous indeed). I have been attracted by Rem Koolhaas's *Delirious New York* for a rather different (and highly idiosyncratic) way of cutting through this ideological double-bind: he *historicizes* the dilemma by transforming "planning" into the unique and historical decision, in 1811, to impose the "grid" on Manhattan: from this single "centralized" decision, then, both the anarchy and the urban classicism (streets and blocks) at once develop.

Robert Venturi, Denise Scott Brown, and Steven Izenour, Caesar's Palace signs and statuary, from Learning from Las Vegas, 1972

Aldo Rossi, Il San Carlone, *1977*

impulse, while still, as the suspicious prefix "post-" suggests, remaining in some kind of parasitical relationship with the extinct high modernism it repudiates; yet what must be explored is the possibility that with postmodernism a whole new *aesthetic* is in the process of emerging which is significantly distinct from that of the previous era.

The latter can perhaps most effectively be characterized (following Althusser's notion of "expressive causality") as an aesthetic of identity or of organic unification. To demarcate the postmodernist aesthetic from this one, two familiar themes may serve as points of reference: the dialectic of inside and outside and the question of ornament or decoration. For Le Corbusier, as is well known, "the plan proceeds from within to without, the exterior is the result of an interior" in such a way that the outside of the building expresses its interior: stylistic homogeneity is achieved thus here by unifying these two opposites, or better still, by assimilating one of them — the exterior — to the other. As for ornament, its "contradiction" with the reality of the wall itself is overcome by the hygienic *exclusion* of the offending term.[33] What may be observed briefly now is that Robert Venturi's conception of the "decorated shed" seeks on the contrary to reinforce these oppositions and thereby to valorize *contradiction* itself (in a stronger way than his earlier terminology of "complexity" or "ambiguity" might suggest). The philosophical formulation of this very different aesthetic move might be found in the (properly poststructural or postmodernist) idea that "difference relates." An aesthetic of homogeneity is here displaced, less in the name of a random heterogeneity, a set of inert differences coexisting, than in the service of a new kind of perception for which tension, contradiction, the registering of the incompatible and the clashing, is in and of itself a strong mode of relating two incommensurable elements, poles, or realities. If, as I believe, something like this characterizes the specific internal logic of postmodernism, it must be seen at the very least as constituting an original aesthetic and one quite distinct from the high modernism from which it seeks to disengage itself.

It will no doubt be observed that the symbolic act of high modernism, which seeks to resolve contradiction by stylistic fiat (even though its resolution may remain a merely symbolic one), is of a very different order and quality from that of a postmodernism which simply ratifies the contradictions and fragmented chaos all around it by way of an intensified perception, or a mes-

---

[33] A somewhat different example of such homogenizing repression can be found in Venturi's account of Frank Lloyd Wright's exlusion of the *diagonal*, in *Complexity and Contradiction in Architecture* (New York: Museum of Modern Art, 1977), 52.

merized and well-nigh hallucinogenic fascination with, those very contradictions themselves (contenting itself with eliminating the affective charge of pathos, of the tragic, or of anxiety, which characterized the modern movement). In this sense, no doubt, Marx's early critique of Hegel's theory of religion retains its force for postmodernism: "self-conscious man, insofar as he has recognized and superseded the spiritual world ... then confirms it again in this alienated form and presents it as his true existence; he reestablishes it and claims to *be at home in his other being*."[34]

I must add to this juxtaposition my feeling that *moralizing* judgments on either of these aesthetics are always the most unsatisfactory way to reach some ultimate evaluation of them; my own perspective here is a historicist one, for which any position on postmodernism must begin by being a self-critique and a judgment on *ourselves*, since this is the moment in which we find ourselves and, like it or not, this aesthetic is a part of us.

That is, however, not the most important point to be made in the present context. One of the more annoying and scandalous habits of dialectical thought is indeed its identification of opposites, and its tendency to send off back to back seemingly opposed positions on the grounds that they share and are determined and limited by a common problematic, or, to use a more familiar language, represent the two intolerable options of a single double-bind. One is tempted to see something of the sort at work here, in the opposition between Tafuri's cultural pessimism, with all its rigor and ideological asceticism, and the complacent free-play of a postmodernism content to juggle the pre-given tokens of contemporary social reality, from which even the nostalgic memory of earlier commitments to radical change has vanished without a trace.

Is it possible that these two positions are in fact the same, and that as different as they may seem at first, both rest on the conviction that nothing new can be done, no fundamental changes can be made, within the massive being of late capitalism? What is different is that Tafuri's thought lives this situation in a rigorous and self-conscious stoicism, while the practitioners and ideologues of postmodernism relax within it, inventing new modes of perception in order to "be at home" in the same impossible extremity: changes of valence, the substitution of a plus sign for a minus, on the same equation.

Perhaps, in that case, something is to be said after all for Lefèbvre's call for a politics of space and for the search for a properly Gramscian architecture.

[34] Karl Marx, *Early Writings*, ed. Bottomore (New York: McGraw-Hill, 1964), 210.

Responses to the Symposium

Some Observations on Writing and Practice

Beyhan Karahan

What is the relationship between critical writing and architectural practice?

Where in the present social and political context does this kind of highly self-conscious writing, which is seemingly unattached to any cultural institution, fit meaningfully into the workings of society? More specifically, how does it inform the practice of architecture?

Is there really a possibility for an "enclave" theory of counterhegemony, as Fredric Jameson proposes, in which a set of "architectural involvements" can be defined?

These three broad questions underlie the following text.

In his conclusion to *Architecture and Utopia*, Tafuri seems unable to visualize the possibility of an architectural intervention based on a set of ideological premises that counteracts the neocapitalist cultural hegemony. The text, in its self-closure in Barthesian terms[1] and its historical determinism,[2] leaves readers in search of an alternative approach, especially those of us interested in the political–ideological implications of architectural practice.

Fredric Jameson suggests the possibility of a "Gramscian alternative."[3] It is clear that the counterhegemony theory developed by Antonio Gramsci still represents one of the less pessimistic approaches to the problem of "culture" to have been posited during the postindustrial era. Given the two different historical and political contexts for the two personalities involved, it is difficult to provide analogous discussions on the same subject

---

[1] See Roland Barthes, *Writing Degree Zero* (New York: Hill and Wang, 1983), 19–29.

[2] The Marxian tradition allows determinism a regulative status as a presupposition of the scientific inquiry. It would be difficult to construct an argument about the deterministic nature of Tafuri's views without substantial background material on his use of utopia and antidialectical nature of some of his thinking regarding capitalist society and culture.

Tomas Llorens, in his article "Manfredo Tafuri, Neo-Avant-Garde and History" (*A.D.* 6/7, 1981), by his method of classification begins to explain the "pessimistic" aspects of "Architecture of Utopia."

In the context of this article, "historical determinism" is used in place of a more descriptive adjective in order to avoid an invented word, and simply refers to the historical irreversibility implied in Tafuri's particular logical construct.

[3] See Jameson's article "Architecture and the Critique of Ideology" in this issue.

matter. Gramsci's and Tafuri's acceptance of the Marxian base-superstructure concept allows them to draw similar conclusions on most general issues,[4] and both theorists provide a cautious treatment of their subject matter. For example, Tafuri criticizes the notion of "architecture for a liberated society" for its utopian overtones and the use of term without any linguistic reexamination. Here his argument is similar to Gramsci's objection to "public spirit," namely that popular myths must be rejected because of their danger of oversimplification.[5]

Tafuri does, in fact, admit the possibility of architectural intervention when and if the unknown parameters in the social forces are resolved.[6] On this point, however, we are in need of more explanation from Tafuri, since the "resolution of social forces" might entail not various stages of advancement of the proletariat revolution but a perfect development of the Keynesian model of capitalist development. The problem begins to develop when one looks for further explanation from Tafuri, since Tafuri relies increasingly on ambiguous approaches in order to describe the cultural phenomena of postindustrialist society. He finds the "ideological function" of architecture to be in a state of crisis, yet opposes the recuperation of partial disclosures of the truth through which a state of consciousness might be achieved — which would probably be the dialectical answer to such a crisis. The relationship between the epistemological and ontological realms is obscured once again as we find ourselves in such difficult logical constructs as being torn between " ... positive objectives and the pitiless self-exploitation of objective commercialization."[7]

In the preceding sentence, even though Tafuri never clarifies what he means by "positive objectives," they are understood to be the opposite of "commercialization" and, most certainly, as Tafuri knows, the answer to the dilemma is not in "wandering restlessly in the labyrinth of multivalent images."[8] In other words, the perceived conflict between the "social good" and "commercial evil" cannot be resolved through formal gestures. This conclusion again takes us back to Gramsci. Its ontological meaning is not in contradiction with Gramsci, yet epistemologically it is very different from Gramsci's treatment of

---

[4] Karl Marx, preface to "A Contribution to the Critique of Political Economy, 1859," in *Selected Works*, vol. 1, 362 – 364.
[5] See Antonio Gramsci, *The Modern Prince and Other Writings* (New York: International Publishers, 1972), 82 – 89.
[6] Manfredo Tafuri, *Architecture and Utopia: Design and Capitalist Development*, 182.
[7] Ibid., 181.
[8] Ibid.

analogous subject matter. For example, we can take Gramsci's criticism of the "economist" approach with regard to an interpretation of the Boulangist movement:[9]

> When a movement of the Boulangist type occurs, the analysis realistically should be developed along the following lines: 1. Social content of the mass following of the movement; 2. What function did this mass have in the balance of forces — which is in process of transformation, as the new movement demonstrates by its very coming into existence? 3. What is the political and social significance of those of the demands presented by the movement's leaders which find general assent? To what effective needs do they correspond? 4. Examination of the conformity of the means to the proposed end; 5. Only in the last analysis, and formulated in political not moralistic terms, is the hypothesis considered that such a movement will necessarily be perverted, and serve quite different ends from those which the mass of its followers expect.

Here Gramsci is criticizing the "economists" for assuming that the mass of the followers of the movement will be so naive as to lose control of the movement. He then concludes that the economist approach reduces political movements to a series of personal affairs. He says that until such movements have actually gained power, it is always possible to think that they are going to fail, like the failure of Boulangism with the use of the Dreyfusand movement. Gramsci's remedy is to continue research directed at identifying the strengths and weaknesses of such movements. His five analytical questions in the passage above provide a logical construct for dealing with the various social implications of political movements.

In other words, economically determined consequences are only one of a multitude of issues relevant to the analysis of any political movement. The French philosopher Michel de Certeau, in his later investigations regarding white-collar opposition to capitalist normative institutions,[10] bases his argument on a different set of issues, and his model appears consistent with

---

[9] See Antonio Gramsci, *Selections from the Prison Notebooks*, ed. and trans. by Quintin Hoare and Geoffrey Nowell Smith (New York: International Publishers, 1980), 129.

[10] Michel de Certeau, "The Oppositional Practices of Everyday Life," *Social Text* 3, 1980.

Gramsci's concept of counterhegemony. De Certeau proposes that because relationships of everyday life bring about a kind of reciprocity between a corporate structure and its workers, the system is obliged "to give" in return for the workers' submission to its rules. He claims that this reciprocity, which in turn is used by the corporate structure in order to "lure," disturbs the fundamental ethics of the system, thereby transforming it. De Certeau's model of everyday life appears to be a useful one for understanding architectural involvements, since these tend to define, program, and formalize the rituals of everyday life in their ultimate realization. (Therefore, perhaps articulating the Gramscian Alternative.)

The following categories of involvement may be enumerated as among the ideological positions most commonly adopted by the "left" within the field of architecture:

1. Architects involved in advocacy planning.

2. Architects involved in community design.

3. Architects opposed to the taking over of natural resources by multinational corporations.

4. Architects concerned with environmental protection, against nuclear warfare, etc.

5. Architects involved in the development of the technical aspects of building construction such as the use of solar energy, less destructive materials, etc.

6. Architects involved in the redefinition of the work force by advocating unionization of architects, establishing a definition of "architectural services," etc.

Beyond these six categories, which primarily relate to the practice of architecture, there are also these:

7. Architects advocating the expression of "higher technology" as opposed to an illusion of styles of the past.

8. Architects responding to formal contextual issues — for instance, the use of regional characteristics in order to maintain the local character of neighborhoods or regions taken over by capitalist, multinational, and real estate interests.

In the categories above, no distinction has been made between architecture as "art" and architecture as "business" — in fact, to do so would most probably lead us into the difficulty of Tafuri's position. By this, we mean that within each category, the interaction between formal and other aspects of political – cultural phenomena requires further investigation. Perhaps one can start by taking each category and looking for a possible "reciprocity" that will cause a reversal of the fundamental ethics of the system.

The role of critical writing, regardless of its limitation resulting from the narrowness of the audience or the difficulty of adaptation by cultural institutions (due to the lack of consensus about the possible conclusions), would be to investigate the exact nature of the intervention within categories similar to the ones listed above. The effectiveness of such writing should be determined by its ability to relate an epistemological understanding to ongoing social and political praxes.

In Reference to Habermas

Jon Michael Schwarting

A critical theory of society requires reference to utopian possibilities. The link between Utopia and critique in Marx's work was part of the logic of explanation. Insofar as a critical social science attempts systematically to uncover the empirical conditions that sustain domination, it must simultaneously formulate the conditions for overcoming that domination. The practical intent is inscribed in the core of critical analysis, if not always explicitly or coherently. A purely "negative critique" is ultimately groundless: a critical theory must justify its normative basis and attempt to elaborate the social possibilities of the human species if it is to have either explanatory or emancipatory power.[1]

Since it has become a familiar practice to examine architecture with respect to other disciplines, most notably the philosophy of language, including structuralism and its successors, it might be useful to discuss the three papers presented at the symposium in relation to the critical – political philosophy of the Frankfurt School. This essay will consider the relationship between the arguments of Fredric Jameson and Demetri Porphyrios and the ideas of Jürgen Habermas, concentrating on the question of whether the architect can carry out significant political action within the limits of his or her métier.[2]

The Porphyrios paper, which owes a heavy debt to the work of Manfredo Tafuri, arrives at a position of ineffectiveness for the progressively oriented architect, ascribing to "critical history" the only operative role. Jameson challenges this position

---

[1] Carmen Sirianni, "Production and Power in a Classless Society: A Critical Analysis of the Utopian Dimensions of Marxist Theory," in *Socialist Review* 54 (September – October, 1981).
[2] In this text I quote freely from Frederic Jameson's "Architecture and the Critique of Ideology," and from Demetri Porphyrios's "On Critical History." The reader may refer to these texts in the pages of this publication.

and suggests a "Gramscian alternative." As opposed as these two arguments seem, both relate to the main themes that recur in Habermas's writing. Central to the work of Habermas, as well as to that of Jameson and Porphyrios, is a concern with the "neoconservative" tendencies of the postmodern condition.[3] Therefore it is valuable to compare the strategies proposed by both Porphyrios and Jameson with those of Habermas, insofar as the three address similar conditions in contemporary culture and society.

Habermas has established a number of essential concepts in his writing since the sixties.[4] Among these are "modern repression," "legitimation processes", and "false consciousness." Whereas both Jameson and Porphyrios apparently concur with most of the analysis of contemporary society from which these concepts are derived, these authors disagree in the conclusions, or predictions, drawn from this analysis. This leaves us with the necessity to draw our own conclusions in order to arrive at a course of action.

Habermas defines "modern repression" as the situation that results from the fact that the prevailing "relationships of power" in society have not been "seen through," and therefore become means of domination. As a consequence, these relationships of power determine the norms and attitudes that we maintain as our "world picture" or "social consciousness." We believe them to be legitimate, that is, accept them as necessary, because of our relationship to a network of institutions and practices of a repressive kind. Architecture is one such institution. For Habermas, this repression furnishes the conditions and the necessity for developing a "critical" and "reflective" type of social science.

Both Jameson and Porphyrios echo this analysis of repression, albeit in slightly different, and possibly crucial, ways. Jameson discusses the problem in more materialist terms, describing the changing "reality of the appearance of capitalism ... which can be called 'late capitalism' or the multinational world system." He describes this new condition as the colonization not only of the Third World, but also of the unconscious, " ... with consumerism, with the enormous penetration and colonization of the apparatus of the media ... mass culture, and the various other techniques of the commodification of the mind." Porphyrios develops the concept of legitimation, extending the

---

[3] See Jürgen Habermas, "Modernity versus Post-Modernity," in *New German Critique* 22 (winter 1981), 3 – 14.

[4] The summary of Habermas's writing has been made from Quentin Skinner's "Habermas's Reformation," in *New York Review of Books* (7 October 1982), 35 – 38.

argument to the realm of architecture. "Reality gives to architecture a set of rules and productive techniques while, in its turn, architecture gives back to reality an imaginary coherence which makes reality appear natural and eternal.... Architectural discourse, in that sense, is totally transparent to ideology."

Within the development of his theory of modern repression, Habermas argues that through repressive institutions and practices a "false consciousness" develops, which causes us to believe mistakenly that restrictive social arrangements are indispensable to our well-being. These beliefs are the source of "frustration," which, for Habermas, implies being prevented or counteracted, and does not mean that other impulses are entirely thwarted or excluded. For Jameson, like Habermas, it is the sense of frustration that permits one to develop theories of change. However, for Porphyrios, as for Tafuri, false consciousness is so pervasive that it leads not simply to frustration, but leads to despair.

Further crucial differences emerge between the positions of Habermas, Jameson, and Porphyrios with respect to their strategies for progressive action. On the basis of his analysis of modern repression, Habermas calls for the development of a "critical" and "reflective" type of social science. This critical process is necessary in order to make us aware of the repressive determinants of our social consciousness; through criticism, the legitimating beliefs will be exposed as having not been rationally acquired. Habermas maintains that once we realize, through critical analysis, that our desires and patterns of social behavior are not our real human interests, we will begin to pursue an authentic understanding of our social situation. Objective knowledge will be obtained once we have reached a condition of absolutely free and unlimited debate. In this state, decisions will be made by "the peculiar force of the better argument." All of this will release us from our previous condition of frustration to be free to enjoy a life of "truth, freedom, and justice."[5]

What could be more utopian? The assumptions that everyone in this new cognitive state will arrive at the same, or at least compatible, truths, that those persons and institutions knowingly perpetrating false consciousness will reform, and that the institutions of the superstructure might so easily be changed are, at best, highly problematic. Habermas is projecting a new world brought about by criticism, clear thinking, and straight talking, as opposed to revolution. Habermas seems to advance these idealistic conclusions as a way of avoiding what Jameson

[5] Skinner, "Habermas's Reformation."

calls Adorno's "late and desperate concept of a purely 'negative dialectic.'"

In contrast to Habermas, Tafuri and Porphyrios consistently work within the terms of the negative dialectic. Porphyrios sees the artist-architect as caught in a process of "mythical structuring that aims at the reproduction of relations of power...because their *raison d'être* is to articulate the relations of power while presenting them as natural and matter-of-fact common sense." This definition of the role of architecture leads directly to certain negative, possibly nihilistic, conclusions. Jameson likens this position to "the Althusserian tradition of 'semi-autonomy' of the levels and practices of social life: politics is radically disjoined from aesthetic practice.... Architects can therefore be political, like other individuals, but their architecture today cannot be political." Thus Habermas's "frustration" appears to be "despair" for Tafuri — despair at the possibility of changing the impending *total system* of late capitalism in which, as Jameson points out, "there can be no qualitative change ... as, for instance, in architecture or urbanism — without beforehand a total revolutionary and systematic transformation." This leads Jameson to conclude, concerning Tafuri's position, that the "sense of Necessity, of necessary failure, of closure, of ultimate unresolvable contradictions and the impossibility of the future ... cannot have failed to oppress any reader of these texts, particularly readers who, as practicing artists, come to them for suggestions and encouragement as to the possibilities for cultural production."

Thus instead of describing the potential role of the architect in either an existing or transformed society, both Tafuri and Porphyrios concentrate on the task of the critical historian. According to Porphyrios, the "critical historian's *raison d'être* is the constitution of architecture as discourse and, in the process of such constitution, the unmasking of the process of mythification wherever and whenever it takes place." This can only be achieved, according to Porphyrios, if "critical history conducts its analysis from outside the discursive site defined by its subject matter. That is the only sense in which it could be said that critical history conducts an objective analysis: objective inasmuch as the critical historian lies outside the discourse that he analyzes." In such a role, as both Tafuri and Porphyrios make clear, this critic can neither practice architecture nor espouse any ideological inclination. As Jameson concludes of this position, "The architectural critic has no business being an 'ideologist'; that is, a proponent of architectural styles of the future, 'revolutionary' architecture, and the like: her role must be resolutely negative, the vigilant denunciation of existent or historical architectural ideologies."

Unlike Habermas, neither Tafuri (in *Architecture and Utopia*) nor Porphyrios wishes to speculate on the consequences of the critical project. Both are resolutely opposed to any possible utopian conclusion. But with no suggestion of how or by whom the critical historian's material is to be used, a number of questions arise, especially if critical history is to remain true to its supposedly anti-utopian position. One set of questions revolves around the problem of the critic's working "outside" the system with no goals beyond the process of demythification. Must the critic's activities, personal and otherwise, also be "outside" to sustain critical purity? Alternatively, can the critic, like the architect, be personally politicized even though his or her work is not? And if society reaches a state of awareness, such as Habermas has described, through, among other things, the work of the critic, does this critic continue to function as such when and if revolutionary action and change take place? Or does the critic switch hats and move from "outside" to an alliance, thereby abandoning critical activity? Or does the critique now focus, from "outside," on the new order as it emerges?

Any expectation that the material produced by the social critic may be used to create a new state of awareness must be considered to be a positive conclusion. However, if one is to extend the Tafurian analysis further, a second set of questions arises, which has less positive implications. Tafuri's and Porphyrios's account of the architect's position in society is based on the notion that the superstructure cannot affect the base. If this is the case, and if late capitalism is so pervasively dominant as not to allow cultural production any role other than that of reinforcing this system (with deviations easily co-opted back into the mainstream), why would the critical historian not be similarly exploited, re-employed, or merely tolerated as ineffectual?

While we may be suspicious of Habermas's idealism, we are, in light of these questions, left by the Porphyrios project with very limited options. If we do not wish to follow Habermas's path into idealism, we need to question Porphyrios's assumption that the critic can remain outside ideology. The assertion that there is no contradiction between the ability to be critical and the necessity to be free of any ideology remains a fundamental issue, and it is here that Habermas and Jameson would disagree with Tafuri and Porphyrios. Like Habermas, Jameson wishes to find an alternative to the negative dialectic. Here again, however, Jameson is more materialistically inclined than Habermas, when he argues for the less utopian, "revisionist" program of the

Gramscian "long march through the institutions" to create a counterhegemony.

By this argument Jameson does not preclude a critical architecture or an alternative architecture. He suggests that this can begin, among a number of possible strategies, "in purely superstructural terms, as the elaboration of a set of ideas, countervalues, cultural styles, which are virtual or anticipatory in the sense that they correspond to a material, institutional base that has not yet 'in reality' been secured by political revolution itself ... or 'enclaves' of small yet strategic pockets or beachheads within the older system."

Taking Habermas's analysis of modern repression as a point of departure, we have arrived at a dialectical proposition. On the one hand, there is the Tafuri-Porphyrios analysis of the imminent "total system" of capitalism, which maintains, in Jameson's description, that "an architecture of the future will be concretely and practically possible only when the future has arrived, that is to say after a total revolution, a systematic transformation of this mode of production into something else." The primary tangible goal for this school of thought must be that of assisting in the perfection of capitalism, and thus hastening its predicted global doom through the "global proletarianism of the work force" (a position that leads Jameson to compare Tafuri's stance with that of Robert Venturi, for whom the by-products of capitalism, the abandoned city, the vacuous suburb, and the strip are "almost all right"). On the other hand, there is Jameson's suggestion, by way of the reference to Gramsci, that the base can be altered by the superstructure. This suggests that cultural production may not be wholly determined, but has the potential to formulate attitudes, to find new means of expressing these formulations, and ultimately to affect the course of societal development. In this view, latitude must be found within the system of "late capitalism" to establish the beginnings of counterhegemonies, whereby alternative systems can be transposed into historically effective mass beliefs and a new ethic. Habermas believes that this formulation was part of the "modern project" and needs revision and continuation, stating that "the project of modernity has not yet been fulfilled." This project aims at a differentiated relinking of modern culture with an everyday praxis that still depends on traditions, but would be impoverished through mere traditionalism. This new connection, however, can only be established under the condition that societal modernization will also be steered in a different direction. "The life world has to become *able* to develop institutions out of itself which set limits to the internal dynamics and to the imperatives of an almost autonomous economic system and its administrative complements."[6]

Such a project requires that a critical analysis be put in its service. For Habermas, to be aligned does not preclude the possibility of objectivity in the analysis of contemporary or historical culture (an idea clearly stated in broad terms by Carmen Sirianni in the passage quoted at the beginning of this essay). Curiously, Porphyrios reinforces this very argument when he makes a momentary departure from Tafuri's argument, stating, "Architecture as ideology has a social function, to insert the agents of an architectural culture into practical and aesthetic activities that support or *subvert* (in varying degrees) the hegemonical power."[7] Although this may be only a Freudian slip, it might well open the discussion in a more fruitful way than rationalizing the pursuit of a critical position "outside" ideology. Might we begin to see a position potentially less nihilistic and more open to the discovery of a mode of effective action within the superstructure? If so, perhaps we ought to attach a Gramscian warning to the Gramscian optimism on which Jameson draws — a warning that advises a careful materialist analysis of, and dialectical reference to, *reality* within any project for change. Nevertheless, it is Jameson's proposal that, although hardly more than a suggestion, permits us to act. Besides its important political implications, it also implies a reintegration of the two forms of thinking: that of *understanding* the nature of things, and that of deciding how to *act* upon them.

[6] Habermas, "Modernity ...," 12 – 13.
[7] My italics.

Theory and Praxis:
Berlin

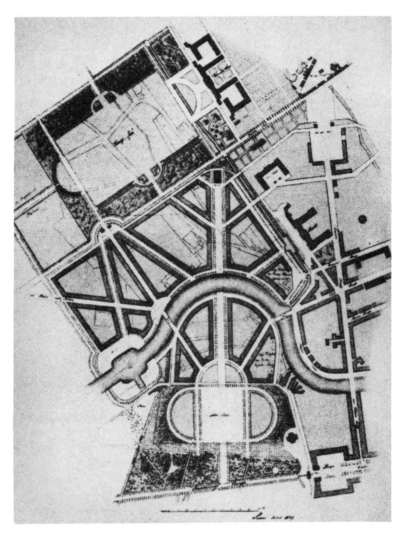

Peter Joseph Lenné, 1839, plan for Moabit and Königsplatz

On Modern and
Postmodern Space

Alan Colquhoun

In these notes I shall discuss urban space in terms of two different ideologies: first, that of the twentieth-century avant-gardes, and second, that of an aspect of the revisionist notions of urban space that has emerged in recent years — the so-called "postmodern" critique.

In doing this I shall use the example of Berlin. My reason for this is that during the last eighty years or so, Berlin has been the site of particularly intense ideological conflict and creative production in the field of architecture and urban planning, owing to special economic and political circumstances. Berlin's tragedy also, in a sense, has been its opportunity.

Let me first of all try to set some limits to what I mean by "urban space." There seem to be two senses in which the phrase is used commonly: in the first, characteristic of geographers and sociologists, the object of study is "social space" — that is, the spatial implications of social institutions, class conflict, and so on. From this perspective, the physical characteristics of the built environment are purely epiphenomenal. They have no real interest in themselves. In the second sense, characteristic of architects, the object of study is the built space itself, its morphology, the way it affects our perceptions, the way it is used, and the meanings it can elicit. This view is subject to two approaches: that which sees forms as independent of functions, and that which sees functions as determining forms. In the latter view, the concept of space will tend to approach that of the geographer and sociologist, though, unlike them, the architect is always finally interested in the forms, however these may be thought to be generated.

The question of the "autonomy" of architectural and urban space — that is, whether forms or functions take priority — has been the occasion of much controversy in architectural discourse since the late eighteenth century. One of the reasons for this is the split that began to open up in the eighteenth cen-

This essay was first presented at a conference entitled *A City: A Conference on Urban Ideologies and Culture in honor of Henri Lefèbvre* at the University of California at Santa Cruz, in March 1983.

tury, with respect to artifacts generally, between the idea of science and that of aesthetics.

Such a controversy would have been meaningless to the Greeks, who were the first in our culture to conceptualize the city as an artifact. In Greek thought the artifact was beautiful if it was well made for a good purpose. The post-Kantian concept of the work of art as a special kind of artifact, which was purposeful but without purpose, did not exist. It is unlikely that the Greeks thought of the city, or even buildings, as objects of aesthetic contemplation in the modern sense. The spatial organization of the city was the result of social and political practice — of action in the public realm. In a certain sense, therefore, the city as an artifact was thought of as an epiphenomenon. It would have made no sense to study it in isolation from the purposes for which it existed. This whole way of thinking is somehow underlined by a fascinating remark by Aristotle — it occurs in *The Physics* and not in *The Poetics*, but nonetheless it has implications for classical artistic theory.

Aristotle says, "If a house were one of the things produced by nature, it would be the same as it is now when produced by art. And if natural phenomena were produced not only by nature but also by art, they would in this case come into being through art in the same way as they do in nature.... Art either completes the processes which nature is unable to work out fully, or it imitates them."

This quotation is part of an argument intended to prove that natural processes do not occur at random, but are purposeful — that nature is teleological, just as human reason is teleological. The distinction we are in the habit of making between nature and nurture has no meaning in this system of thought. The city, as an artifact, is both natural and rational, and in both cases is inscribed in a teleology.

With the rise of the historicist outlook in the late eighteenth century, however, what was "rational" and therefore "natural" in classical thought became increasingly dubious. In the subsequent Marxian development of this new attitude, what was "rational" was seen as ideology — opinion and not science. Beauty, which had been underwritten, as it were, by absolute reason, was now seen as contingent, subjective, and relative. But at the same time, in reaction to this skeptical relativism, a new idealism emerged, which attributed to beauty a transcendental status. Idealism and historical relativism were two sides of the same coin. We are still in this debate, and it has a strong bearing on the idea of urban space. Modernism tended to take a historicist and relativist view of architecture and to regard the city as an epiphenomenon of social functions, resulting in a certain kind of urban space. But postmodern developments tend to disengage urban space from its dependence on functions, and to see it as an autonomous formal system. This view indeed may accept that all art is ideology, but it maintains that ideology always operates with a limited number of rhetorical and artistic devices, which are not mere symptoms of the ideologies that make use of them. It therefore insists that we must discuss urban space in terms of these rhetorical and artistic strategies, which are independent of any simple historical determinism.

Before going on to discuss specific examples of contemporary urban space in terms of these two concepts, I would like to touch on the word "space" itself, as used in architectural discourse. The notion of an entity that we can call "architectural space" is relatively new. It was probably first formulated by the German aesthetician and art historian August Schmarsow in the 1890s as a critique of the theory of stylistic development put forward by Heinrich Wölfflin in his book *Renaissance and Baroque*. Schmarsow's definition of space is strictly phenomenological and psychological. Before Schmarsow, everyone had been perceiving architectural space without realizing it, rather like Monsieur Jourdain had always been speaking prose. But although in one sense all Schmarsow did was to categorize something that had "always existed," in another sense he changed people's way of interpreting architecture quite radically. Space was now a positive entity in which the traditional categories of tectonic form and surface *occurred*. Henceforth architects would think of space as something preexistent and unlimited, giving a new value to ideas of continuity, transparency, and indeterminacy; so that when we use the apparently harmless word "space," we have to be aware of its ideological implications. It is not a neutral expression. And as I will show, it is precisely this idea of an abstract, undifferentiated "space" that has been one of the main objects of attack by postmodern urban criticism.

With this caveat in mind, let us now look at urban space, using a narrative on Berlin to investigate two themes: 1) the space of social housing, and 2) the space of the urban public realm.

Nothing illustrates more clearly the genesis of what one might call modernist urban space than the social housing in Berlin and other German cities in the 1920s. It is well known that the liberal and socialist avant-garde architects of the 1920s rejected the perimeter courtyard housing block in favor of free-standing parallel slabs. There were intermediate solutions, in Vienna, Amsterdam, and Berlin itself, in which the perimeter block and the street were retained, but cleared of all internal building to provide spacious interior courts, such as the well-known Karl Marxhof in Vienna. And one should not forget the French solutions of the early twentieth century, like those of Eugène Hénard, where the courtyard was turned inside out and opened up to the street to provide light and air.

But on the whole the modernists of the 1920s rejected these solutions as "compromises," and the seried ranks of parallel slabs à la Hilberseimer and Gropius, spaced according to angles of light, became the norm — especially in the Germany of the Weimar Republic, though also in Holland, in the second phase of the Amsterdam plan, and in various projects of the Italian rationalists.

I believe we must see this typology as a direct answer to the *Mietkasernen*, which had been hurriedly built in German cities in the last third of the nineteenth century to house the rapidly increasing urban proletariat. When one sees these *Mietkasernen* today, with their incredibly high density, and their labyrinthine and squalid courtyards, one suddenly understands the whole modern movement. Today, both in West Berlin, where they are occupied by Turkish immigrants, and in East Berlin, where they are occupied by native Germans, these *Mietkasernen* are still in use, and their slumlike condition is exaggerated by the total lack of maintenance. This shows how patchy the impact of the urban ideals of the modern movement has been on the structure and morphology of the old cities, except in areas where considerable wartime destruction has taken place — and this is true even under regimes in which the state controls all real-estate development.

The Berlin *Siedlungen* or "housing estates" of the 1920s, constructed under the general supervision of Martin Wagner and Bruno Taut, were built, as I just said, as a critique of the *Mietkasernen*. They are halfway between garden cities and urban *quartiers*, mostly (though not always) situated on the periphery of the city, often near industrial areas, and served by public amenities.

The garden city movement had a profound impact in Germany in the years immediately preceding World War I. Several suburban sites were laid out in Berlin on principles derived from Camillo Sitte. The 1920s *Siedlungen*, like their immediate garden city forebears, were no longer thought of as extensions of the city grid, as the new nineteenth-century housing area had been. They were seen as self-contained model suburbs, consisting of three- or four-story walk-up apartment slabs, set in semirural surroundings.

Unlike the garden city estates, the new *Siedlungen* did not exhibit symmetrical axes or spatial containment. They consisted

Ernst May, Siedlung Römerstadt, Frankfurt-am-Main, 1927—1928

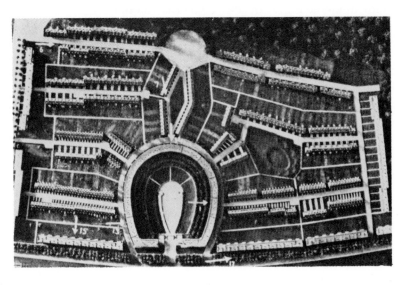

Bruno Taut and Martin Wagner, aerial view of Grosssiedlung Britz, Berlin, 1925—1931

of mechanically arranged *series* of parallel blocks, and were deliberately *sachlich*; that is, they were antisentimental and "scientific" both in layout and iconography — smooth white surfaces, flat roofs, repetitive slabs. The whole operation, from the arrangement of the slabs to the organization of the standard apartment plans, was influenced by the management theories of the Americans Taylor and Ford.

Nonetheless the architects who designed them retained many of the "humanistic" ideas of the previous, more "artistically" oriented generation (although many of them were indeed apostates of this very generation, including of course Bruno Taut himself). There are many examples of spatial manipulation to create recognizable order and enclosure, including centrally focused spaces like Taut's horseshoe scheme in the Britz Siedlung, and the long curved wall of apartments in Siemenstadt. There is also much attention given to variety of design, composition of solid and void, and a highly sensitive use of materials and color to mediate the effect of regularity, monotony, and abstraction. Especially today, after fifty years of planting, many of them do not at all resemble Hilberseimer's diagrammatic "negative utopias." In fact, in many ways they seem to belong more to the ethos of the Arts and Crafts movement than to the post-World War II modernist housing estates we are now used to.

The main feature of these 1920s *Siedlungen* that survived World War II was the concept of the building slab in space as opposed to the perimeter block — a figure-ground reversal of the traditional city, with its solid fabric cut through with streets. Otherwise, these relatively dense, small-scale layouts were abandoned for higher slabs with elevators, widely separated, occupying a no-man's-land of open space. This approach was characteristic of social housing in Western Europe and some North American cities (notably New York City) after World War II. It was also a feature of the post-Stalin era in East Berlin, when whole sections of the inner city were razed and replaced with widely spaced ten-story slabs.

If we take these developments as a whole, from the 1920s to the 1960s, we have to ask the question, does the avant-garde represent a continuing humanizing and ameliorative attention toward the space of social housing, or are there other, less utopian factors at work? With this question we are at the heart of the problem of modernism, with its blowing apart of perceptible urban space, its insistence on high-rise housing, and the precedence it gave to fast automobile circulation. It seems that what started as a utopian critique of nineteenth-century housing conditions turned into nothing more than what was needed for the success of twentieth-century economic centralism, whether in the form of monopoly capitalism or socialist bureaucratic control. This raises the whole problem of the unbridgeable gulf between what the individual can perceive and feel at home in, and the vast, abstract infrastructural network that is necessary for the operation of the modern consumer and media-based society. Modernist city planning has destroyed the possibility of symbolizing the social public realm, and has created a polarity between an increasingly minimal private space and a public realm that defies any kind of spatial representation.

This leads me to my second theme: space of the urban public realm. There is a sense in which the avant-garde of the 1920s denied the distinction between the public and private realms, if only because it was mostly concerned with the problem of social housing on the urban periphery and the creation of self-contained dormitory areas.

But this tendency of the twentieth-century avant-garde to ignore the public realm was balanced, in the early years of the twentieth century, by its very opposite: gigantic, baroque-style and purely honorific urban spaces symbolizing the state. Examples of this include the Washington Mall as redesigned under the McMillan plan of 1901; Lutyens and Baker's New Delhi; Canberra; and Albert Speer's plan for the new north-south cross-axis of Berlin.

The pretentiousness and vulgarity of Speer's plan and its political associations should not blind us to the fact that it belongs to a characteristic early twentieth-century typology used by democratic, socialist, and fascist regimes alike. It belongs to what has been called the "reinvention of ritual" in the late nineteenth and early twentieth centuries.

Nor was the Speer plan created in a vacuum. It was the culmination of a large number of abortive projects from the early nineteenth century onward for developing a north-south axis across the Tiergarten, with its head nestling in the conveniently concave loop of the Spree. The Reichstag, which now stands surrealistically like a stranded whale in the middle of the most derelict part of the Tiergarten, near the Wall, was a part of this historic development. Speer's scheme was not only the culmination of this tradition, but also a way of linking the north and south railroad stations. It therefore had the Haussmannesque purpose of creating an important circulation route between the two parts of western Berlin historically isolated from each other by the wedge of the Tiergarten.

To these examples must be added Stalinallee in East Berlin, where there is a curious fusion of baroque ideas and socialist

Stalinallee, East Berlin, 1956

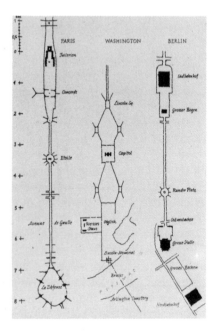

Diagrammatic comparison of the Champs-Elysées, Paris; the Mall, Washington, D.C.; and the major north-south axis of Berlin, shown to the same scale

Karl-Marx Allee, East Berlin, 1963

Albert Speer, proposed north-south axis for Berlin, begun 1937

housing. The main route into Berlin from the east is an operation à la Haussmann, the high walls of housing being shaped to provide visual climaxes along the triumphal entry to Berlin.

It was only Le Corbusier, within the twentieth-century avant-garde, who ambiguously tried to bridge the gap between a socially functionalized city and the city as symbol of civic or national identity and power — as is shown by his projects for Paris, Rio, Algiers, St. Dié, and the realized projects of Brasilia and Chandigarh.

But in the 1950s CIAM took up, for the first time within the modern movement, the question of the city core — the unprogrammed traditional city center, forming a new category not covered by the previous categories: living, working, recreation, circulation.

One of the most significant (if indirect) results of this new departure was the competition for the *Hauptstadt* Berlin in 1957, in which Western architects were invited to submit plans for the eighteenth-century downtown area of East Berlin. Leaving aside the political gesture this competition represented — the notion that Berlin would be reunified *as part of the West* — we can perhaps see this competition as a riposte to Stalinallee, and as a countersymbol of "democracy and modernity."

All the schemes were demonstrations of the principles of modernist urban space, now accepted as the ideal reflection of welfare-state capitalism. They consisted of object-type buildings isolated from each other, or forming series, in a neutral and limitless space, arranged around the great axis of the Unter den Linden, and connected by transportation networks. Most of the schemes were vaguely Corbusian in inspiration — Corbusier himself submitted a scheme — with those of Hans Scharoun and Peter and Alison Smithson making some sort of "organicist" counterpolemic. Scharoun's scheme was like a giant children's play scene, designed by a gigantic child, without any sense of the scale of the city. The Smithsons' was equally out of scale, with its raised pedestrian walkways often one hundred meters wide and about three kilometers long, spreading over the town like a constantly growing cobweb. It is one of the earliest examples of those nodal megastructures that became so popular in the 1960s. In all the schemes the surviving historic buildings were preserved but left stranded, like the Reichstag is today, as isolated museum fragments dwarfed by the new buildings and transport networks.

A little earlier, the city architect of East Berlin, Hermann Henselmann, in his post-Stalin mood, began erecting housing slabs in the area south of Stalinallee (by now renamed Karl Marx Allee) on Western models.

Le Corbusier, plan for restructuring the center of Berlin, 1958

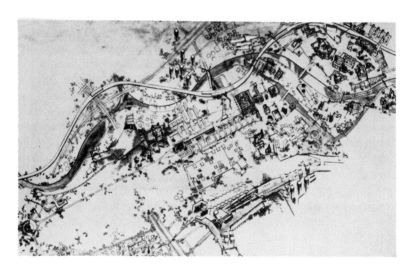

Hans Scharoun, plan for restructuring the center of Berlin, 1958

But in recent years — and this underlines the curiously symbiotic relationship between East and West Berlin — there has been, on both sides of the Wall, a massive reaction against these modernist urban ideas. In a sense, there has also been a reaction in the East (or so it would appear) against the monumental ideas espoused by Stalinism — ideas which, as we have seen, had a certain amount in common with those of Speer and Hitler. These rejections, however, are not total. The modernist city has been rejected insofar as it postulated urban space as limitless and abstract, and was based upon the theoretical separation of the different functional elements of the city. The monumental city has been rejected insofar as its aim was propagandist and its style megalomaniacal. But, as Tafuri and Dal Co have rightly said in connection with Stalinallee, "It would be wrong to regard what resulted as purely ideological and propagandist; in reality Stalin-allee is the fulcrum of a project for urban reorganization affecting an entire district ... in fact, it succeeds perfectly in expressing the presuppositions for the construction of the new Socialist City, which rejects divisions between architecture and urbanism and aspires to imposing itself as a unitary structure."

In East Berlin there recently has been an exhibition of plans for the reinstatement of the gridded street pattern and the urban block over a large area of inner Berlin. Instead of trying to create grandiose symbols, the intention seems to be to reinforce and extend the traditional institutional center of the city. This intention is also shown by the fact that East Berlin is now in the process of renovating and reconstructing the eighteenth-century monuments in the historic center. (There has even been some collaboration between East and West; recently West Berlin returned to the East the sculptural figures designed by Schinkel for the bridge across the Spree at the top of the Unter den Linden.)

At the same time the West Berlin *Internationale Bauaus-stellung* — IBA — has inaugurated a series of schemes for rebuilding in the derelict area near Checkpoint Charlie. This project is also based upon the urban block as the basic unit of urban morphology. These projects are more modest in scale than those of East Berlin and differ from them in planning logistics. In the West a number of sites have been distributed to well-known architects and local developers, whereas in the East, as one might imagine, there is a concerted master plan, with variety and indi-viduality restricted to facade treatment. (Large-scale concrete prefabrication is now being used to produce "classical" and "art deco" facades, in a way that suggests that, if we talk of "postmodernism," it is a postmodernism that has strong connec-

Werner Düttmann, Hans Müller, Georg Heinrichs, plan for the Märkische residential district, Berlin, 1962 – 1965

Emilio Battisti and collaborators, proposed IBA housing for Lutzowplatz, Berlin, 1980

tions with the older tradition of socialist realism. The projects being designed in the West are less literally historicist in their facades, only very generalized references, in the neorationalist manner, being made to classical or vernacular traditions.) One of the disadvantages of the planning procedures of IBA is that blocks by different architects and in different styles face each other across the streets, so that the street itself is not unified. But for all their problematic features, I think we can see in these developments a welcome new concept of the space of the public realm. The main thrust of this new tendency is to reconstitute the city as a continuous urban fabric. It rejects the notion that every program type has its equivalent type-form. It rejects the CIAM classification of the city in terms of the differentiated generic functions — living, working, recreation, transportation — with its rigid concept of zoning and its denial of multivalency.

Instead, it seems to suggest a classification of the city in terms of a number of possible formal types or strategies: 1) It sees the city, with its perimeter blocks and streets, as a solid, anonymous fabric that should contain a variety of functions, including housing and commerce. 2) The few isolated buildings, whether old or modern, would gain symbolic importance by contrast with this continuous fabric. 3) It reinstates the street and the public square as the places of unprogrammed public enjoyment and congregation, encompassing both the consumer and the *flâneur*. 4) It reinforces the pedestrian scale and rejects the dominance of fast, motorized circulation. 5) It sees the public space of the city as more analogous to so many external rooms, with definite boundaries, than to a limitless void within which buildings, circulation routes, etc., occur. 6) Finally, it conceives of the city as historically continuous — capable of being read as a palimpsest. In the early twentieth-century avant-garde, the city was seen diachronically, as a linear development over time, each period canceling the one before in the name of the unity of the *Zeitgeist*. The revisionist view looks at the city as the result of temporal accumulations in space, a sequence in which the latest intervention takes its place.

This is one of the most potent models of urban space to have replaced the 1920s utopia. Against this we must set not only the urban utopias of 1920 to 1970, but also the actual modern city, where the image is one of chance, competition, profit, and corporate power. In spite of its chaos — which is alternatively seen as "stimulating" and "alienating" — this city tends toward specialization, thus bringing to pass one of the aims of the 1920s avant-garde. The city proper is the place of work and commerce. Private life takes place in the rural suburbs. Thus the modern city sustains a schizophrenic image of the individual, who is one person in his own work situation, and quite another at home. It encourages the view of modern life as dominated by simulacra.

The revisionist model, in fact, is more tolerant of the existing city than of the utopias of the classical avant-garde, precisely because the actual city is confused and congested. Nonetheless it implies a degree of conscious ideological commitment and architectural order, which runs counter to the actual city. This view has been criticized as representing a regressive utopia (equal and opposite, perhaps, to the modernist utopia), based upon a nostalgic image of past culture. This criticism would surely be justified if what was being presented were a literal model of the past, which might easily decline into kitsch, or at best (to the extent that it was realizable on any substantial scale) be nothing more than a formal solution incapable of being infused with life and appropriated socially.

But to say that the past cannot simply be repeated, to acknowledge that modern life has its own exigencies, which are the equivalent of those that gave the traditional city its original meaning, is not the same as saying that modern society's break with the past is so complete and inexorable that no traditional social or artistic values whatever can be relevant to it. To suggest this would be to return to the modernist conception of a fully determinist history, in which the past has simply to be blotted out. In this debate, *all* such absolutist arguments are pointless, since they are based upon purely logical antinomies whose consequences are built into their premises.

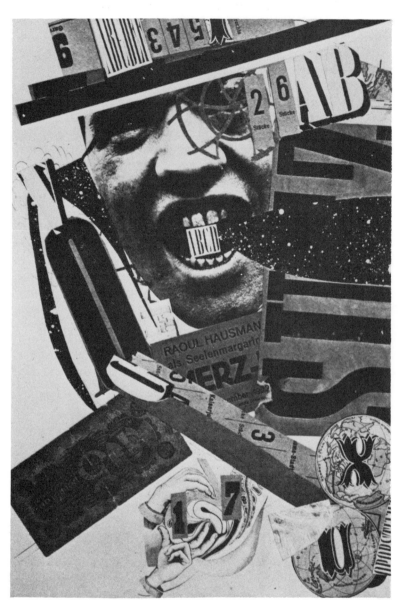

Raoul Hausmann, ABCD, photomontage, 1920−1923

Introduction

The following text is a complete translation of the fourth chapter — actually, the fifth if the elaborate theoretical introduction is considered as a chapter — of Manfredo Tafuri's *La sfera e il labirinto: avanguardie e architettura da Piranesi agli anni '70* (Turin: Einaudi, 1980). The chronological boundaries marked by the subtitle (from Piranesi to "postmodernism") indicate the extensive itinerary Tafuri charts for himself in tracing the history of the avant-garde and in elaborating the ways in which the signifying practices of the negative avant-gardes come to be installed within the institutional domain of architecture as a "language of transgression" that, in turn, comes to be codified and "consumed."

To negotiate the dense and perhaps off-putting skein of allusions at work in the opening paragraphs of this excerpted chapter, the reader should bear in mind that Tafuri attempts both to recapitulate the theoretical position elaborated in the introduction to the book and to redirect the historical analysis of the pre-avant-garde and of avant-garde theatrical practices forged in the first three chapters. He casts his historical analysis in the methodological form of a Nietzschean genealogy — or, to be more precise, an archaeology, along the lines of Foucault — concerned with the analysis of the discursive formations of architecture. Crucial to Tafuri's genealogy and the "other" history of the avant-garde within architecture it seeks to document is the role accorded to Piranesi as precursor of the twentieth-century avant-gardes and negative prophet of the modern metropolis. Therefore, the present chapter following two chapters dedicated to the radical, anti-Enlightenment reading of Piranesi and another chapter concerned with the deployment of the metropolis as a mise-en-scène in futurist and expressionist theater, constitutes an attempt to explore the ideological and "linguistic" implications of the adventures of the avant-garde in their unfolding within and across the regimes of capitalism and socialism as represented by Weimar Germany and postrevolutionary Russia. The chapter meticulously prepares the groundwork upon which will be constructed, in three successive chapters, specific analyses of the interaction between the avant-garde and various architectural establishments in their national contexts: the U.S.S.R. of the first Five Year Plan, the United States on the threshold of the New Deal, Weimar Germany in the grip of *Sozialpolitik*.

Tafuri is difficult to read not only by virtue of the modernist and postmodernist modes of writing he employs and the diverse critical methodologies at work — and, at times, at odds — in his text, but, more important, because he conceives of the historical project as the "project of a crisis." If historiographic work is to assume a critical productivity, it must, according to Tafuri, set into crisis not only its subjects and their plurality — in the case of *La sfera e il labirinto*, the linear history of the avant-garde must be dismantled in order to contest a certain monumental history of architecture and architectural culture — but also the historical project itself and the critical operations and the languages of history it employs. The very productivity of Tafuri's text lies, therefore, in the precipitation of its own crisis, a crisis to be shared ultimately by the reader, who will find himself caught in the labyrinth of Tafuri's writing of history *in the plural*. Among the critical positions Tafuri deploys are the following: the genealogy/archaeology of Nietzsche/Foucault, the deconstruction of Derrida, the critical thought of the Frankfurt School and the *pensiero negativo* of its Italian offshoot, and, most important, the Marxian interpretative framework — de-vulgarized and modernized — that governs the entire project, always binding to a specific *historic space* the negative work of breaking up texts and works. It should, however, be remarked that this setting into collision of critical discourses and positions is a technique for troubling "reality," for probing the fault lines between reality and ideology. As Tafuri writes, "The real problem is how to project a criticism capable of constantly putting itself into crisis by putting into crisis the real."

Such a critical project is particularly efficacious in the writing of architectural history, where a constellation of diverse practices must be distinguished and the specific history of each must be constructed according to archaeological means. The great strength of Tafuri's architectural writing lies in its ability to reconstruct the specific ways in which architecture, techniques, institutions, urban administration, ideologies, and utopias come together in the textual site of a particular work, formal system, or even an unrealized work or fragment. The privileging of the unfulfilled architectural project — for example, Piranesi's engravings viewed as projects *manqués* — and of aesthetic programs — the archaeology of the avant-garde manifesto undertaken in the following text — is symptomatic of Tafuri's genealogical work in general: that "meticulous and patiently documentary work" that, in Foucault's definition, "operates on a field of entangled and confused parchments, on documents that have been scratched over and recopied many times."

Pellegrino d'Acierno

U.S.S.R. – Berlin, 1922:
From Populism to
"Constructivist International"

Manfredo Tafuri

If the history of the theatrical avant-gardes seems to unfold with a certain linearity, it is nevertheless necessary to point out the contradictions within the very concept of the avant-garde that manifest themselves as moments of rupture — as moments of conflict that emerge along the problematic boundary line separating the avant-garde itself from the reality principle. It is on that shifting line that the space without places of the avant-garde tries to cover its tracks. And it is this game of hide-and-seek between necessity and freedom that nullifies the Nietzschean discovery of the free acceptance of the necessary as the unique and supreme freedom. Seated in the orchestra, the pre-avant-garde — and we are dealing here with the *flâneur* of impression-ism, but also with the symbolist caught up in his feverish nights — could make its own peregrinations within Piranesi's *Prisons*, incarnated in the nineteenth-century metropolis, the provision for a regression to the happy optics of childhood. Climbing onto the stage, the "baby Don Quixote" forces himself to enumerate his own cruel, destructive impulses. Exposing himself stark naked, he is forced to admit what Sade and Pira-nesi, in different ways, had announced to the world: that where the logic of assassination has taken over, the greatest pleasure is in being simultaneously torturer and tortured; that it is useless to wander through the city looking for the guilty one, inasmuch as "guilt" is found in the flesh and blood of the prisoner as well as the imprisoner; that the devastation wreaked on linguistic insti-tutions appears first as grotesque farce, then as tragedy. By making a code of such infractions, mountains of rubble will be obtained. I can limit myself to heaping these fragments into piles, to manipulating them into assemblages poised between utopia and heterotopia, to forcing once communicating signals to react to the incongruous juxtaposition to which I oblige them; but the very fact that I express this desire to assume the guise of the

This chapter of *La sfera e il labirinto* (Turin: Einaudi, 1980) is printed here with the kind permission of the author.

121

executioner "represents," and only represents, the fiction of my fabulations. Cruel as they may be, they remain within the enclosure where I keep them. The space separating them from the chain of events that, despite everything, transforms each deconstruction into a new universe of discourse is infinitesimal.

Why should we be surprised, then, if, in the early 1920s, there was an attempt to confront with institutional structures the logic, perfect in itself, of the illogical? If the attempt was made, that is, to transform the "bridge" uniting the devastated language with the reality that reduced it to such a state into a "door," suddenly thrown open onto the extreme boundary that divides and rejoins object and subject?[1]

From this perspective, will the organization of the intelligentsia be aligned as fellow traveler or as alternative to the political organization? The problem had already been at the center of German *Aktivismus* in the years around 1910, but it changed dimension when confronted with the historic drama of the October Revolution.

On one side, there was the tradition initiated by Pinthus and Pfemfert with the proposal, in 1911, for a "world office" that would "unify all of the humanitarian tendencies that run in parallel but disorderly directions, and bring about a concentration and a promotion of all creative activities."[2] On the opposite side, there was the ambiguous alliance between the formalist school and the constructivist avant-garde, which presented itself to the public as the homology of the October Revolution. The clash between these two hypotheses of political hegemony could only have taken place in Berlin — there where the revolution in the councils, defeated, could still "speak" through the pages of *Die Aktion*, opposing the KPD with the same antibureaucratic themes used to confront Social Democracy.[3]

The encounter between the German and the Soviet avant-gardes thus took place in a climate of certainties clashing with anxieties: it was the very function of the intellectual that was now at stake, both for the artists in the West, who were trying to safeguard their existence in the face of the world of capitalistic non-value, expressed in all its brutality during the years of inflation after the war, and for the artists in Russia, facing the new

[1] We use here the terms "bridge" and "door" with the metaphorical significance attributed to them by Georg Simmel in "Ponte e porta," in *Saggi di estetica* (Padua, 1970), 3–8; original ed. "Brücke und Tür," in *Der Tag*, 15 September 1909.

[2] *Die Aktion*, 1911, no. 3. See Giancarlo Buonfino, *La politica culturale operaia. Da Marx e Lassalle alla revoluzione di Novembre. 1859–1919*. (Milan: Feltrinelli, 1975), 170 ff.

[3] Ibid., 175.

problems posed first by wartime communism, and then by the NEP. Berlin, on the other hand, had for some time been historically designated as the meeting place between the East and the West. In Berlin, Diaghilev, through the "painting in motion" of his Russian Ballets, had promulgated the image of an uncontaminated Eastern "spirituality," and a similar function was performed by the Russian artists of the Blaue Reiter and their guests — Kandinsky, Goncharova, Larionov, David Burliuk, Kasimir Malevich — who had exhibited their work in 1919 at the Herbst-Salon, and by the one-man shows of Archipenko and Chagall, organized by Herwarth Walden at the Sturm. It was the very same cultural climate that, in the first years after the war, had dominated interest for Russian art.

Nevertheless, the impact of the first official manifestations of Soviet art in Berlin in 1921–1922 cannot be understood unless we take into account the particular tension dominating German avant-garde circles between 1917 and 1920. The reaction against the catastrophe of the war, the revelation of the violence of the institutions of the European bourgeoisie, the intellectual excitement aroused by what came to be called the "November Revolution," and the prospect glimpsed of a "new world" generated by the emergence of the popular masses as political protagonists were appraised quickly by German intellectuals as new terrain for ideological construction. As a specific terrain, that is, that would restore meaning to intellectual work itself.

The old program of the Die Aktion group now seemed to have been legitimized by historic events: caesuras between ideology and political action, in the name of a populist impulse heir to the eschatological expectations of prewar expressionism, could no longer exist.[4]

[4] "Let us traverse the arena of art!" Grosz and Wieland Herzfelde would write in 1925, "Movement, publicity, noise; but also noble isolation, resignation, and escape from the world, individual versatility even in the halls of Academe.... Who has the true idea of art? *Der Sturm; Der Kunstwart; Der Cicerone;* or *Kunst und Künstler; G; Das Kunsblatt?*... No era has been as hostile to art as that of today, and if one, referring to the average man of today, were to state that he can live without art, he would be exactly right.... Today's artist, if he doesn't want to be an idler, someone who is obsolete and wandering blindly, can only choose between technique and the propaganda of the class struggle. In both cases he must give up pure art. Either siding, like the architect, engineer, or designer of advertising posters, with the army — organized, unfortunately, in a very feudal manner — which develops the forces of industry and exploits the world; or showing the face of our time, representing it and criticizing it, as a propagandist and defender of the revolutionary idea and of its supporters, and siding with the army of the oppressed, who struggle for their rightful share of the world's goods, for a judicious, social organization of life." George Grosz and Wieland Herzfelde, "Die Kunst ist in Gefahr" (Berlin, 1925), now in Diether Schmidt, *Manifeste, Manifeste 1905 — 1933* (Dresden: Verlag der Kunst, 1965). Note, however, that Grosz's atti-

Ludwig Meidner closed his pamphlet *An alle Künstler*[5] with these words: "It is a question of socialism — meaning justice, freedom, and love for one's fellow man, *the divine order of the world*"; and his words were echoed in Max Pechstein's statement, "Art to the people and the people to art *through work.*" Work as an ethical redemption, then, as a new "antibourgeois" value, as a "richness" specific to the proletariat. The traditional hopes placed in the revolutionary role of the "conscious producers" were all gathered together by the postwar German messianism. It was not by chance that in 1919 Kurt Pinthus defined socialism as the "Great dawn of humanity, gravedigger of a decaying world! Guide to the earthly paradise!" The appeal to the "obscure masses," of pure expressionist imprint, was counterbalanced by the promise of a new *peace.*[6]

Karl Jakob Hirsch, writing in 1928 in the special issue edited by Will Grohmann, *Kunst der Zeit: Zehn Jahre Novembergruppe*, recalled the atmosphere that arose during the war within the group of artists engaged in the inspection of aerial troops; among them was Georg Tappert, one of the most active coordinators of the Novembergruppe:

> It all began in the inspection office of the aerial troops, so similar to an atelier, where painters dressed as soldiers were supposed to reproduce aircraft. Under their desks, however, lay revolutionary drawings by the talented Pfemfert for the *Aktion*, done on Prussian Imperial sheets of paper with Prussian Imperial ink. Here were born *Die schöne Rarität* and some of the *Roter Hahn*. They winked a circumspect eye at the demonstrating workers as a sign of sympathy in January of 1918, and they stayed shut up there waiting for the hour of liberation, *because the light shone from the East.*[7]

tude toward the U.S.S.R. and the Soviet avant-gardes is extremely ambiguous and changes with time. See Irwin Beth Lewis, *George Grosz: Art and Politics in the Weimar Republic* (Milwaukee – London: Univ. of Wisconsin Press, 1971).

[5] Ludwig Meidner, "An alle Künstler, Dichter, Musiker," in the pamphlet *An alle Künstler*, edited by the W. Simon art gallery (Berlin, 1919), with essays by J. R. Becher, L. Meidner, Bernhard Kellermann, Max Pechstein, Walter Hasenclever, Kurt Eisner, Konrad Haenisch, Kurt Erich Meurer, and Paul Zech, and reproductions of works by César Klein, Hans Richter, Lyonel Feininger, Georg Tappert, etc.

[6] Kurt Pinthus, "Rede an die Weltbürger," in *Genius. Zeitschrift für werdende und alte Kunst* (Munich: Kurt Wolff, 1919), 167.

[7] Karl Jacob Hirsch, "Novembergedanken," in the pamphlet published by Will Grohmann, *Kunst der Zeit: Zehn Jahre Novembergruppe*, special number of the

The *light that shone from the East* was clearly the light of social peace, of "realized Jacobinism." This is evident in the rough draft of the *Manifesto of the Novembrists*, in the manifestos of the Hallische Künstlergruppe, of the Vereinigung für neue Kunst und Literatur of Magdeburg, of the groups Der Wurf and Bielefeld, of the Rih-Gruppe of Karlsruhe, not to mention the most noted program, of the Arbeitsrat für Kunst:

Art and religion.
The world's people become holier through them. Freer in brotherhood. Greater in their thrust toward loftier heights. The liberator of us all: ART.[8]

The people and art must form a whole. The artist with his work will create the space in the Absolute for the regeneration of his heart.[9]

Freedom of the subject, as a corrective and confrontation to the conservative social art practiced with the unstable ethic of commercial interests. Freedom and authentic life for the individual.... It wants to transcend the commonplace, which means freedom from it. It tends to recognize the forms of expression of counter-art, that is to say, of the art of those regarded as infantile or as sick, according to its own laws, not as a rational product of consciousness, but rather

review *Kunst der Zeit. Zeitschrift für Kunst und Literatur*, III, no. 1 (1928), 18. On the history of the Novembergruppe, see the documentation in the volume of Helga Kliemann, *Die Novembergruppe* (Berlin: Mann, 1969), and Rudolf Pfefferkorn, "Die Novembergruppe, Programme und Weg," in *Die Novembergruppe* (Berlin, 1977), 5–23. On the artistic environment of postwar Germany, see John Elderfield's essay "Dissenting Ideologies and the German Revolution," in *Studio International*, vol. CLXXX, no. 927 (1970), 180–187, and the essays by Aaron Scharf, "John Heartfield, Berlin Dada and the Weapon of the Photomontage," ibid., vol. CLXXVI, no. 904 (1968), 134–139; Manuela Hoelterhoff, "Heartfield's Contempt," in *Artforum*, vol.XV, no. 3 (1976), 58–65; Eckhard Siepmann, *Montage: John Heartfield vom Club Dada zur Arbeiter–Illustrierten Zeitung* (Berlin, 1977); and, naturally, the documentary inventory published in the *Almanacco Dada*, ed. Arturo Schwartz (Milan: Feltrinelli, 1976). See also the volumes of Benjamin Goriély, *Le avanguardie letterarie in Europa* (Milan: Feltrinelli, 1967), 234 ff. (the chapter "Dada in Germania"), and Luigi Forte, *La poesia dadista tedesca* (Turin, 1976). Among the autobiographical memoirs, it is interesting to compare the one from the conference held on 1 October 1971 by Huelsenbeck at the ICA — Richard Huelsenbeck, "Dada or the Meaning of Chaos," in *Studio International*, vol. LXXXIII, no. 940 (1972), 26–29 — with Raoul Hausmann, "Courrier Dada" (Paris, 1938). Finally, see Hanne Bergils's article, "Dada Berlin," in *Tendenzen der Zwanziger Jahre* (Berlin, 1977), vol. III, 65–74.
[8] Appeal of the Vereinigung für neue Kunst und Literatur, in Kliemann, *Die Novembergruppe*, 59.
[9] Appeal of the group Der Wurf, Bielefeld; ibid., 59.

as an expression subjected to its own particular laws.[10]

We find ourselves on the fertile terrain of the revolution. Our motto is LIBERTY, EQUALITY, FRATERNITY. Our union is derived from the equality of our human and artistic conceptions. We consider it our highest duty to dedicate ourselves totally to the spiritual edification of the young, free Germany. We fight for the worthwhile in every field and we support our intention with all the means at our disposition. We therefore ask for an unconditional adhesion and a definite stance on the part of the public.... We are neither a party nor a class, but men, men who work untiringly in the space that Nature has assigned to them: at work which, like all other work for the good of all the people, must find favor with the general interest and needs the esteem and recognition of the masses.... Our struggle is directed at all the forces of disintegration, our love at all the forces of construction. Our sentiments are young, free, pure. Our uncontaminated love goes out to the young, free Germany; we want to combat with courage and without hesitation the backwardness in it with all the forces at our disposal. We send to all cubist, futurist, and expressionist artists, conscious of their mission, our fraternal greeting with the hope that they will unite with us.[11]

A complete fusion of art and people, and "struggle against the forces of disintegration": the Novembergruppe, the Arbeitsrat für Kunst, and the Bauhaus of Weimar all agreed on this generic program (for another reason as well: to a large extent, the various groups ended up with the same protagonists). Thus, the Berlin dada proclaimed itself an enemy of the pacifism of that which came to be called the "O-Mensch-Bewegung," and Raoul Hausmann, Hannah Höch, Hans Richter, George Grosz, and Hans Arp joined in with the Novembergruppe, together with the Sturm painters, with Enrico Prampolini, and with Kurt Schwitters.

The utopian and humanitarian populism that shaped the activist, antiwar, and messianic wing of the second German

[10] Catalogue of the group Rih, Karlsruhe; ibid.
[11] "Manifesto dei novembristi" (draft), in Grohmann, *Kunst der Zeit*, 16.

George Grosz and John Heartfield, Dada-merika, *1919*

expressionism can, in fact, be recognized in an October Revolution interpreted — by the West — as the epiphany of the Spirit self-fulfilled in the proletariat. For Bruno Taut, too, the "new world," the "day of peace," appeared on the horizon of the East; but the "new world" glimpsed by him was the one dreamed of by utopian expressionism, the one evidenced by the ambiguous projects presented at the competition for the "House of Friendship" in Istanbul (1916) or by the projects for the "City of Peace" designed by César Klein, Kampffmeyer, Schmidt-Rottluff, and Taut himself.[12]

It was not by chance that Robert Michels had been a collaborator in the Aktion, and that from the beginning Rosa Luxemburg and Karl Liebknecht were its political points of reference, just as Tolstoy and Kropotkin had been guarantors of the "fraternity" (*Brüderlichkeit*) of which Hiller and Rubiner had become the apostles. The antibureaucratic stance, inherited from the Aktion, gloried in the Tautian utopism. But the improbable synthesis of subjective consciousness and the utopian collectivism of Taut had already been enunciated by Lu Märten, who in 1911 had written:

> It is not the individual who creates, awakens, and ultimately expresses the unprecedented forces and demands of a new content of life; on the contrary, the longing, the thrust, the thought, and the demands that ... increasingly coalesce give birth to that Only One, that Superman, that dream now become flesh and blood, who discerns in the chaos of the present a conscious creation and, eventually, a form.[13]

The Only One thus coincided with the dream: only the dream was capable of "conscious creation" within chaos. Rubiner, for his part, in 1912 prescribed "intensity, wisps of the fire of intensity, its bursting out, its shattering into pieces, its explosion. Its spurting forth, its assassinating, its proof of the extreme unforgettableness of a single instant."[14]

The "longing for catastrophe" was a reaction to the threat that *Zivilisation* had hurled at the Spirit:

> Once the great bewilderment caused by technique is overcome, because it has become

[12] See Barbara Miller Lane, *Architecture and Politics in Germany, 1918–1945* (Cambridge, Mass.: Harvard Univ. Press, 1968); Kurt Junghanns, *Bruno Taut* (Berlin: Henschel Verlag, 1970).

[13] *Die Aktion*, no. 2 (1911).

[14] Ludwig Rubiner, "Der Dichter greift in die Politik," ibid., nos. 21–23 (1912).

accepted as an obvious thing, there is no difference in principle between the *Iliad* and *Die kleine Stadt* of Heinrich Mann. At least, not in the principle, which is close to the *Iliad*.[15]

And it is logical that this was so for one who could accept, as did Lu Märten, that the Supreme One was Christ, or — as for Yvan Goll — a Chaplin burdened with the sorrows of humanity: sacrifice was called for to guarantee a synthesis capable of connecting millenary cultures and apocalyptic expectations. The Christ-Superman was certainly not the Zarathustra who, as a "last sin," tried to teach "superior men" to mock themselves. On the contrary: he was the prophet of a regression, or better, of a repression. Within the symptomatic experience of this conflict, there was concealed a supreme desire for peace. Antibureaucratism ended up in the longing for eighteenth-century anarchies. Here too the decomposition showed its constructive side; but the hoped-for cosmic revolt of the Only One was mirrored in the mysticism of Blok's *Twelve*.

The City of Peace of the German utopians was, in essence, the expression of the utopia of the *city of social peace*: in this, the radical artists rejoined the humanitarian socialism of Berlage, who in 1915 planned his Enlightenment-like Pantheon of Humanity, or the subsequent projects of Le Corbusier for the Mundaneum, which aroused, not surprisingly, the criticism of Karel Teige.[16] The Bolshevik revolution, in fact, was seen as the realization of the Temple to Humanity, as the realization of the fullness or the purity of the ideology of the Enlightenment, as a synthesis of Jacobinism and petit-bourgeois anarchism. Rousseau plus Kropotkin plus Tolstoy equals Lenin: this was the synthesis more or less unconsciously proposed by the heirs to the activist pole of expressionism. A synthesis that remained alive, but with different ends, in the organs of the opposition groups that grew up in Berlin during the course of the war, and that were to converge in the Berlin dada: from the Café des Westens, to the journal *Neue Jugend* of the Herzfelde brothers, to *Die Freie Strasse* of Raoul Hausmann and Franz Jung.

It was in this atmosphere of excess that Adolf Behne could give life to his utopia of *architecture as a natural absolute*: as a

---

[15] Ibid.

[16] On the Le Corbusier-Teige dispute regarding the Mundaneum, see George Baird, "Architecture and Politics: A Polemical Dispute. A Critical Introduction to Karel Teige's 'Mundaneum,' 1929, and Le Corbusier's 'In Defense of Architecture,' 1933," in *Oppositions* 4 (1974), 80 ff. But also compare Marcello Fagiolo, "Mundaneum 1929. La nuova Babilonia secondo Le Corbusier," in *Ottagono*, no. 4 (1978), 22 – 29.

collective action aimed at the recovery of a creativity that was an end in itself, *free from the slavery of necessity*, free from the alienating weight of technology. The architecture of Oriental temples was indicated by Behne as a model to be followed, as the expression of a complete communion of man with his fellows, and of society with nature. A communion, moreover, explicitly considered as an anti-European cultural motif (anti-intellectualistic, that is) and, in a broad sense, laden with protesting values; the romantic anticapitalism of the early Behne can be found, after all, in the Gropius of the years from 1917 to around 1922.

The recent philological inquiries made by Pehnt, Klotz, and Franciscono have in fact thrown sufficient light on the characteristics of this period of Gropius's research — a period not by chance carefully downplayed by Gropius himself, who, from 1923 on, was intent on imparting a totally mythic dimension to the German experiences of the early 1900s.[17]

Pehnt's archival research has brought to light the joint project of Behne, Gropius, and Bruno Taut, who, together with J. B. Neumann, planned the magazine *Bauen* — the first issue of which was to appear in June 1919 — directed not at specialists but at the "people," and with the specific intent of contributing to the "victory of true socialism." It was Gropius himself, after all, who at the inaugural conference of the Arbeitsrat für Kunst declared, "I think of our organization as a conspiracy [*Verschwörung*].... Our goal is a new *Spirit*, which, once created, will lead to new achievements."[18]

The utopia of the "cathedral of the people," created by the hands of millions of workers, thus united, in the postwar Gropius, with the romantic idea of the *Bauhütte* executed with Adolf Meyer near Berlin for Sommerfeld. The inaugural ceremony for the Sommerfeld house was deliberately conceived by Meyer as a mystical ritual, in the very same tradition of the sacral rite with which Peter Behrens and Georg Fuchs had inaugurated the cenacle of art of Ernst Ludwig von Hessen in Darmstadt.

The communion between human work and the cosmos posited by Adolf Behne was also interpreted by Gropius, who recognized in wood — bear in mind that Sommerfeld, his client, was the leader of Germany's wood industry — the material in which the mystical union between people and nature could be

---

[17] See Wolfgang Pehnt, "Gropius the Romantic," in *The Art Bulletin*, vol. III, no. 3 (1971), 379–392; Heinrich Klotz, "Materialen zu einer Gropius-Monographie," in *Architectura*, no. 2 (1971), 176–196.

[18] Walter Gropius, Inaugural Conference of the Arbeitsrat für Kunst, typescript in the Bauhaus-Archiv, cit. in Pehnt, "Gropius the Romantic," 380.

found. Glass — the synthesis of matter and the immaterial, the symbol of the transparency of the subject with respect to collectivity — should be used only when the "new man" — Toller's "naked man" — knew autonomously and collectively how to build with it his own future "cathedrals of socialism."[19]

It is clear that, apart from some tangencies that definitely exist (and that we shall not fail to point out), such mystical populisms, descendants of the apocalyptic dreams of social regeneration of Mühsam, Pinthus, and Rubiner, and in general of the intellectuals grouped around Herwarth Walden and the gallery and the review *Der Sturm*, were objectively antithetical to the activist and provocative idealism of the dada group.

It is necessary, therefore, to go back to the historical sources of this antithesis. Indeed, one cannot ignore the fact that the motto that opened the manifesto of the Novembrists — "liberty, equality, fraternity" — merely repeated the themes of the propaganda apparatus set into motion on a vast scale by the Social Democratic party after 1890. All the means of mass communication, as Buonfino shrewdly demonstrates,[20] were used by the party, on the authority of the ideologies of Kautsky and Bernstein, to evoke the *Geist* of class solidarity. But this solidarity, for Kautsky as for Engels, was an instrument of organization in the name of a mechanical transformation of the great trust into a rough draft for socialist society. If, in fact, the *Konzernes* had as their ineluctable *destiny* — as Kautsky theorized — a plan aimed at their "natural" elimination, the *brotherhood* of the proletariat, and of the masses of farm workers subordinate to industrial production, was not so much a political antidote as the corrective that could "humanize" that unstoppable and fatal process. Not surprisingly, Bernstein dwelled on the instruments of universal suffrage and on consumer cooperatives — rather than on those of production, which to him were antithetical to socialism — reducing the action of the party to pure "movement," without an immediate goal.

The centralization of cartels was thus for Bernstein a means of control of the market and of arbitrary adjustment of production and of prices. To the theory of collapse promulgated by Rosa Luxemburg, Bernstein counterposed a capitalistic harmony at the interior of which any action by the state could only be a disturbance. The orthodox wing of the party, on its own, followed the expansion of proletarianization in order to seize its

[19] See W. Gropius, "Neues Bauen," in *Der Holzbau*, supplement to no. 22 (1920) of the review *Deutsche Bauzeitung*.
[20] Buonfino, *La politica culturale*, passim.

immediate political advantages. But the purpose and the line of march of this split between politics and economy remained indefinite. For Kautsky, the development was to be neither interfered with nor supported: all that was necessary was to remedy "its ruinous and degrading consequences."[21] Buonfino has written perceptively,

> The mythology of the class in itself was simply the froth of the political program for democratic planning: and incredibly it became the substance of the thesis of the opposition on the left — Kautsky was opposed by the extreme left with the instruments that he himself had forged ... the concepts of "avant-garde" and of "working-class spontaneity" were inherent to the elevation that Kautsky had elaborated in terms of "class in itself," immanent in history and in the social universe, and thus perfect and autonomous. This mystification, once accepted, implied that the only political task be that of *liberating it from organization*; this would have let loose in all its *pure violence* a total antibureaucratism against the state, against capitalism, but also against the workers' party.[22]

This explains why the groups of independent socialists (PUS) and of anarchists headed by Wille and Landauer were able to propose the sacralization of the *Geist* against every form of organization. The attack on the workers' party was thus conducted simultaneously with that on the state plan. The colonies of leftist artists and writers that propagated by imitating the living conditions of the proletariat certainly had adopted as their model the medieval "immaculate knight." But in practice they transformed Lassalle's and Kautsky's ideology of "brotherhood" into an antibureaucratic protest. *Die Aktion* would assemble these aspirations into a totality, trying to form an alternative to the powerful Social Democratic culture industry. But its humanism of dissent would become trapped on the terrain of Kautskian ideology. As for the Berlin dada, it could also lash out against the activists, calling them "exhausted men, beating time to and singing psalms through streets in which escalators run and telephones ring," who resurrected the sick fable of "humanity."[23]

[21] Karl Kautsky, *La questione operaia* (Milan: Feltrinelli, 1971), 365.

[22] Buonfino, *La politica culturale*, 129.

[23] *Dada-Almanach* (Berlin: Eric Reiss, 1920), now in Schmidt, *Manifeste, Manifeste*, 192, and in *Almanacco Dada*, 201.

George Grosz, Automaton Republicans, *1920*

Jefim Golyscheff, Untitled, 1919

But was the metropolitan experience lived as merely a moment, as a "non-significant *Erlebnis*,"[24] as a momentary accident, this reduction of the individual — exalted and ridiculed at the same time — to a nullity, really antithetical to the Social Democratic pedagogy regenerated by Landauer's philosophy of spontaneity?

Certainly the harmonic synthesis of Weimar was rejected by the "living for uncertainty" of dada. But now the field of comparison was no longer the humanitarian sermon of the Social Democratic *Bildung* or the *Schau*, the vision, of Rubiner, but the "new organization" that Russia made a reality in 1917.

It is significant that the contacts with the Soviet artistic experiments in the years immediately after the October Revolution closely followed these premises. The example of Jefim Golyscheff is a case in point. Golyscheff, who was born in Cherson in 1897 but lived in Odessa until 1909, went to Berlin to study music. Interested in architecture, painting, and chemistry, he played in the Odessa Symphony Orchestra. From 1911 to 1913 he toured as a violinist; as he himself wrote, he witnessed "the coronation at Delhi, the war in Tripoli, the Chinese revolution in Canton, and November 9, 1918, in Berlin." It was Behne who "discovered" the Russian artist, who was exhibiting at the "show of unknown architects" in Berlin.

In his paintings and drawings, Golyscheff approached a kind of abstract and naive expressionism. Not only for this reason was he suited perfectly to becoming a model of the "revolutionary artist" in the eyes of the Berlin avant-garde, but also because of the lighthearted, ironic, and at the same time experimental character of his work. In fact, he invented new musical instruments and created happenings of a dadaist flavor; it must also be remembered that in 1914 he worked out a dodecaphonic system, which, some have claimed, even influenced Thomas Mann in the writing of his *Doctor Faustus*.

Golyscheff's intense experimentalism was totally in keeping with the feverish Berlin experiments of the years immediately following the war. In 1919 he exhibited his work with the Novembergruppe at the Grosse Berliner Kunstausstellung, but quickly became a part of Berlin's dadaist group, as Raoul Hausmann recalls:

[24] In *La politica culturale*, 197, Buonfino writes that "Dada was ... a modern version of Schiller the educator (circuses for the illumination of the proletariat); dada was the *Platonic* operation of a plastic imitation of the perfect form of the *god;* the non-significant *Erlebnis*. The accidental was no longer wicked (as Vischer had said) except with regard to the reality of the *formal revolutionary idea par excellence*, and Lassalle had already emphasized this in his *Sickingen*."

One day, in the spring of 1919, I met a young man by the name of Jefim Golyscheff. If there exists some doubt as to whether the dadaists were truly dada, there was none in Golyscheff's case. He did not have to inquire about the opinions held in dada circles; he possessed innately all the qualities of the authentic dadaist. Like Caesar, he came, saw, and conquered.... At the first dada exhibition, in April 1919, he showed things never before seen: jam jars, tiny bottles, pieces of wood, scraps of plush, locks of hair. An optical shock; there had never been such a presentation.... The first dada exhibition at the Graphischen Kabinett opened with a gala evening, in which Golyscheff appeared together with a young lady dressed in white. I can still see this scene today, as though it were yesterday. Golyscheff, holding back a laugh, goes to the piano, with a slight movement of his hands sits the innocent angel down, and with the voice of an electronic doll, says: "Antisymphony part 3a / = guillotine of musical war / a) provocatory spray, b) chaotic oral cavity or the underwater airplane / indissoluble Hyper-Fis-chen-dur." ... His astute mechanical art, on the edge of acrobatics, snatched from the artfulness of music uncanny sounds, so unexpected that they transported the mind to infratonal vertigoes.[25]

Even Behne underlined, with the populist coloring often found in his essays of the period, Golyscheff's experimentalism and the hymn to the "joy of protelarian work" contained in it:

[Golyscheff] brings little, touching elements — nuclei, seeds of a new art.... With sheets of paper colored and pasted together, with note paper, he creates something original.... A Russian and an iconoclast, with his drawings intended for the proletariat, he wants to incite his viewer to the joy of producing, even in the area of the simple and charming. There is altruism in Golyscheff's art, an art that he feels to be "communist."... An art of the elementary, of that which is the *most human [Menschlichsten]*.[26]

[25] Raoul Hausmann, "A Jef Golyscheff," in *Phases*, no. 11 (1967), quoted in Eberhard Steneberg, *Russische Kunst in Berlin 1919–1932* (Berlin: Mann, 1969), 11.

Golyscheff's Berlin experiments thus represent the vitalistic and "positive" pole of dada tendencies. Far removed from the self-destructive mysticism of Hugo Ball or Johannes Baader, he embodied, between 1919 and 1922, an intellectual figure totally in keeping with the typology of the "Russian artist" dear to the German avant-garde in their messianic expectation of the "horizon of peace" coming from the East.

In this sense, his well-documented relations with Bruno Taut and the group dominated by Taut were clearly decisive. At the exhibition of the Unbekannte Architekten, Golyscheff presented an urban system with residential buildings for two thousand families, hospitals, concert halls of glass, and bridges of various heights — one of the customary utopian images through which the artists of the Glass Chain expressed the desire for a pure state of planning. It is more important to point out other, more original motifs that appear to have been absorbed by Taut: the "theory of colored architecture," being in effect an explosion of the oppressive urban structures as well as an invitation to a "reconstruction of the universe"[27] and to a liberating and anticonventional collective behavior, is so close to the vitalist and naive dadaism of Golyscheff that it becomes legitimate to suspect a concrete relationship between his work and that of Taut.[28] Moreover, it must be pointed out that, for both, the invitation to a self-liberating behavior was explicitly directed at the proletariat, the only historical subject capable — for them — of making its own the "gay science" of purifying devastation.

This was so to the point that Golyscheff, in polemic with the manifestos then proliferating in Berlin, published his own leaflet, A-ismus, directed against seriousness and in favor of gaiety. Still another Nietzschean motif, in the purest dada tradition. And it is important to point out that Golyscheff's A-ismus was answered in the pages of Frühlicht by Taut's "Nieder der Seriosismus"[29] — further proof of an exchange of experiences, merged in

[26] Adolf Behne, "Werkstattbesuch bei Jefim Golyscheff," in Der Cicerone, 1919.

[27] The reference to the famous manifesto of Balla and Depero, Ricostruzione futurista dell'universo, is intentional. It is undeniable that there are notable affinities between the work of early futurism and that of the immediate postwar period in Germany. Taut's experiments in Magdeburg and, still earlier, the excessive utopism of the Gläserne Kette and of the Unbekannte Architekten have their historical origins in the work of prewar futurism. See, for example, Gino Severini's manifesto, Le analogie plastiche del dinamismo. Manifesto futurista, of September–October 1913, now in Archivi del futurismo (Rome, 1958), vol. I, 76–80.

[28] Note that the project presented by Golyscheff at the Exhibition of Unknown Architects was preserved in Magdeburg by Bruno Taut. See Steneberg, Russishe Kunst in Berlin, 12. On Golyscheff, see also the catalogue of the exhibition dedicated to him by the Museum of São Paulo, 1965, and D. Gojowy, "Golyscheff, der unbequeme Vorläufer," in Melos, Neue Zeitschrift für Musik, no. 1 (1975), 188–193.

the complex kaleidoscope of the Berlin avant-garde.

It is evident that the importance of Golyscheff's moment in the spotlight of the Berlin dada and in the circle of the Arbeitsrat für Kunst should not be overestimated, especially since as far as our study is concerned, the bond between the avant-garde and populism as embodied by Golyscheff is a completely fortuitous one. On the other hand, the very same Arbeitsrat was to reveal itself to be anxious for a considerably more institutional bond with the innovations, especially those on an organizational level, then underway in Soviet Russia. Nor must it be forgotten to what an extent the Berlin groups — from the Arbeitsrat to the Novembergruppe, up until the Ring — had as one of their primary objectives a relationship between avant-garde experiments and national and municipal institutions (educational, administrative, and commercial).

Not surprising, then, is the attention paid by the Arbeitsrat für Kunst to the "Artistic Program of the Commissariat for Popular Instruction in Russia," published in the *Kunstblatt* (no. 3, 1919), and submitted by Ludwig Baer to the members of the Arbeitsrat for discussion. Baer also furnished additional material of Soviet origin to the Kiepenhauer publishing house in Potsdam, which in 1920 published the first German work on the Russian avant-garde, *Neue Kunst in Russland, 1914 bis 1919,* by Konstantin Umansky, an author who also wrote essays on Kandinsky and on Tatlin's Monument to the Third International for Munich's avant-garde review *Der Ararat.*

Eberhard Steneberg has compared the *Artistic Program* of the Soviet commissariat with the first Bauhaus manifesto (Weimar, 21 March 1919).[30] The attention that Gropius directed to the new Soviet educational institutions was of a contradictory nature, however. The entire early period of the Bauhaus, in fact, appears — after the more recent philological and documentary rereadings[31] — considerably more like the ultimate proof of a

---

[29] See Bruno Taut, "Nieder der Seriosismus," in *Frühlicht,* supplement no. 1 of the review *Stadtbaukunst alter und neuer Zeit,* 1920. Now in Ulrich Conrads, *Programs and Manifestoes on 20th-Century Architecture* (Cambridge, Mass: MIT Press, 1970), 57, original ed. *Programme und Manifeste zur Architektur des 20. Jahrhunderts* (Frankfurt – Berlin: Ullstein, 1964).

[30] Steneberg, *Russische Kunst,* 9.

[31] See Francesco Dal Co, "Hannes Meyer e la "venerabile scuola di Dessau, " introduction to Hannes Meyer, *Architettura o rivoluzione* (Padua: Marsilio, 1973); Walther Scheidig, *Bauhaus, Weimar, 1919 – 1924* (Liepzig: Edition Liepzig, 1966); the essays of Ezio Bonfanti and Massimo Scolari in the special issue of *Controspazio* dedicated to the Bauhaus (II, no. 4 – 5 [1970]); Marcel Franciscono, *Walter Gropius e la creazione del Bauhaus* (Rome, 1975), with an introduction by F. Dal Co, original ed. *Walter Gropius and the Creation of the Bauhaus in Weimar* (Carbondale, Ill: Univ. of Illinois Press, 1971); Karl Heinz Hüter, *Das Bauhaus in Weimar: Studie zur*

"flight from the world" attempted by an intellectual coterie anxious to protect itself from urban anguish than the logical premise to what would later become the mythical aspect of the Bauhaus itself. The fact is that in 1920 Gropius became acquainted with Kandinsky, from whom he obtained the program of the Inchuk.[32] In this way new themes began to circulate within the Bauhaus environment — from the analysis of the specific means of artistic communication, to the influence of forms on the public, to the relationships between formal structures and behavior. Kandinsky's psychologism — of German origin, after all — thus began to disturb the mystical vitalism of Itten's *Vorkurs*, and an early project for the restructuring of the school was given as the reason for the summoning of Kandinsky himself by Gropius. But apart from this personal relationship, there is no doubt that for Gropius and for the new masters of the Weimar Bauhaus, the mysticism of the "cathedral of the people" was reflected in a millenarian and eschatological interpretation of the October Revolution. In this sense, there was no contradiction between the flight into the Goethian city — the explicit symbol of an incurable nostalgia for totality, for the fullness of experience, for the integrity of values — and the attention (more than just feigned) to the

Gesellschaftspolitik. Geschichte einer dt. Kunstschule (Berlin: Akademie Verlag, 1976); various authors, "50 Jahre Bauhaus Dessau," in *Wissenschaftliche Zeitschrift der Hochschule für Architektur Bauwesen Weimar*, XXIII, no. 5−6 (1976).

[32] See Kurt Junghanns, "Die Beziehungen zwischen deutschen und sowjetischen Architekten in den Jahren 1917 bis 1923," in *Wissenschaftliche Zeitschrift der Humboldt-Universität*, no. 3 (1967), 369−370. As further evidence of the interest shown by German intellectuals in the new Soviet institutions, it may be useful to cite the letter sent to Lunacharsky in the spring of 1920 by Professor G. Kornelius, director of the Munich School of Art, together with the proofs of his book *La nuova pedagogia artistica*. Kornelius wholeheartedly commended the social renewal of the world and stated that, knowing full well Russia's problems at that moment, he would nevertheless willingly accept an invitation from the Narkompros as a teacher in the State Higher Studios. See A. Lunacharsky, "Novaya khudozhestvennaya pedagogika," in *Khudozhestvennaya zhizn*, no. 4−5 (1920), 17. However we must also take into account the inverse influence, that of the German avant-gardes on the Russian ones, after 1917. Starr has revealed that Melnikov owned a handwritten translation of Bruno Taut's *Stadtkrone* (1919) and of Paul Scheerbart's *Glasarchitektur* (1914), observing that the semireligious ceremonial planned for the burial vault designed by the Russian architect in 1919 is rightly included within the expressionist current, while the project, rejected by the Committee, for the glass sarcophagus for the body of Lenin (1924) draws its origins from "crystal architecture." Melnikov himself was to praise the vital energy contained in the acute angles of his project for the sarcophagus. See S. Frederick Starr, "Kostantin Mel'nikov, architetto espr ssionista?" in *Lotus International* 16 (1977), 13−18. Naturally, one can also rea 1 Melnikov's symbolism the legacy of Russian millenarianism, by no means unknown to artists such as Khlebnikov or Malevich. Melnikov's expressionism in the Rusakov Club was recognized as derived from Mendelsohn in Michajl Ilin's article "L'expressionisme en architecture," in *L'architecture d'aujourd'hui*, no. 2 (1930), 29−31. See also S. Fr. Starr, *Melnikov. Solo Architect in a Mass Society* (Princeton: Princeton Univ. Press, 1978).

new Soviet experiments.

And so we are still in the atmosphere of a worn-out populism: in the same climate that impelled Taut to cite — alongside Kropotkin's anarchic theories on the dissolution of the city and the formation of integrated communities of production and consumption — Lenin's decrees on the socialization of the land;[33] in the same climate of the declarations of faith in the creative force of the people published by Gropius in that significant document, the *Deutscher Revolutionsalmanach;*[34] in the same perspective of waiting for an ethical revolution evidenced by the Berlin avant-garde, a typical example being the dada manifesto of Huelsenbeck, Hausmann, and Golyscheff.

It is precisely the latter document that offers the occasion for establishing an exact watershed between the populism of the early Bauhaus and the Berlin dadaist ethic: two ways, in effect, of reacting to the shock of 1917.

The manifesto of the Central Dadaist Revolutionary Committee was divided, as we know, into three fundamental points:

> 1) The international revolutionary union of all productive and intellectual men and women on the basis of a radical communism.
>
> 2) The progressive elimination of work, achieved by means of the mechanization of every type of activity. Only through the elimination of work would it become possible for the individual to achieve certainty, authenticity of existence, and integrity of experience.
>
> 3) The immediate expropriation of wealth (socialization) and its transfer to the community; the subsequent creation of *cities of light*, whose gardens would belong to the entire society and would prepare man for the state of freedom.[35]

[33] Bruno Taut, *Die Auflösung der Städte* (Hagen: Folkwang Verlag, 1920). Note that the Leninist law on land was also published in W. C. Behrendt's review *Die Volkswohnung* in 1919.

[34] Walter Gropius, "Baukunst im freien Volkstaat," in *Deutscher Revolutionsalmanach für das Jahr 1919* (Hamburg – Berlin, 1919).

[35] See the leaflet published in *Der Zweemann*, no. 2 (1919), 18 – 19 (now in *Almanacco Dada*, 130), and Richard Huelsenbeck, *En avant Dada: Eine Geschichte des Dadaismus* (Hanover – Leipzig – Vienna – Zurich: P. Steegemann, 1920). The positions of Huelsenbeck and Hausmann with regard to political commitment were, however, anything but consistent: "Dada," wrote Huelsenbeck in *Dada-Almanach*, page 3 (*Almanacco Dada*, page 243), "is the American side of Buddhism; it shouts because it is able to keep quiet, it acts because it is at rest. Dada is thus neither politics nor an artistic tendency, it votes neither for humanity nor barbarity, 'it contains in its toga war and peace, but it chooses the Cherry Brandy Flip.'" For

It is difficult to find — among the numerous political testimonies of the European artistic groups of these years — a more paradigmatic document of a completely idealistic interpretation of the Bolshevik revolution and of the first decrees of socialization emanating from Lenin. But it also reflects, even though indirectly, the antibureaucratic polemic conducted in Germany by Rosa Luxemburg. Among the jumble of themes emerged the following: a) the prospect of a universal epiphany caused by the cosmic embrace between intellectuals and the people; b) the fundamental theme of a *freedom from work* brought about by the acceleration of technological innovation — a freedom that must overflow into human behavior, into a regained collective ethic; c) the theme, again, of the *city of peace*, seen as a ludic instrument of education to the new freedom achieved.

This political program — whose novelty for the worn-out intellectual consciences of successive generations intent on "saving their souls"[36] it is useless to emphasize, as does Coutts-Smith, given that the entire avant-garde experience is subject to cycles and recurrences — we have said was completed by Huelsenbeck, Hausmann, and Golyscheff, with further, paradoxical requests: the daily provisioning of intellectuals and workers, the obliging of priests and teachers to subscribe to the "dadaist articles of faith," the adoption of a simultaneous poem as a state prayer, the organization of one hundred and fifty circuses "for the illumination of the proletariat," "the immediate regulation of sexual relations in compliance with the principles of international dadaism and through the institution of a dada sexual center."

□

his part, Hausmann wrote in *Der Dada*, no. 1 (1919), 3 (in the *Almanacco Dada*, 159−160): "There isn't one damned man of letters who isn't already independent and a communist. Communism is like shoe polish — ten pfennigs a liter, and this guarantees you a safe-conduct pass. It is the masses that compel these wretches, who formerly went to the greatest extremes in their self-discipline. Certainly the masses are materialistic, not spiritual. We are against the spirit. Thanks, in the name of the worms.... The masses don't give a damn about art, or about the spirit. Nor do we. Which doesn't mean that we are trying to look like a temporary commercial company of communism. The atmosphere of the cattle market (the German revolution) is not for us." It should further be noted that Huelsenbeck's article "Der neue Mensch," written for the *Neue Jugend*, marks a temporary break with dadaism, extolling the strength of one's own soul (perhaps ironically) in terms of sexual strength. Cf. *Dada, Monographie einer Bewegung*, ed. W. Verkauf, M. Janco, and H. Bollinger (Teufen, n.d.), 61, and Forte, *La poesia dadista tedesca*, 81−82.

[36] See Kenneth Coutts-Smith, *Dada* (London: Studio Vista, 1970).

The politicization of the Berlin dada differentiates it sharply from the original Zurich dada or that of Paris. In the manifesto of the Central Committee of Dada, in the clownish parades in neighborhoods still riddled by Noske's bullets, in the leaflets written by the Herzfelde brothers, Walter Mehring, Hannah Höch, Georg Grosz — *To Each His Own Football, Bankrupt, Adversary*, etc. — we can see the break between the heterogeneous Berlin group and the lucidly self-destructive legacy of the "negative utopia" so tragically embraced by Hugo Ball. Mehring recalls:

> In the streets lined with gray barracks, marked by the bullets from the battles of Spartacus and lacerated by the howitzers of the Noske regime, our group was received with applause and shouts of joy, while we performed somersaults or marched to the rhythm of sentimental songs such as *Ich hatt' einen Kameraden* or *Die Rasenbank am Elterngrab*. After the cannibalesque dances of the putsch of Kapp, much more savage than those of Sophie Tauber's marionettes, after the *danse macabre* of the Stahlhelm movement and its swastika ornaments, which seemed to have burst out from a Hans Arp *Heraldry*, our dada procession (*Jedermann sein eigner Fussball*) was greeted with a joy as spontaneous as the *on y danse* of the Paris mob before the Bastille. The phrase "to each his own football" became popular in Berlin as an expression of anti-authoritarian and demystifying contestation.[37]

It may seem paradoxical, but it was actually through the intervention of the least politicized of the Berlin dadaists — and of that isolated dadaist, Kurt Schwitters — that the experiments of Soviet constructivism conquered an ambiance such as that of Berlin, still so bound up with the last ferments of expressionist humanitarianism. The famous photograph taken at the 1920 dada fair in Berlin, showing George Grosz and John Heartfield with a placard extolling the tower of Tatlin — "Die Kunst ist tot / Es lebe die neue Maschinenkunst / TATLINS" — documents expressively this period of transition. "Art is dead": this was the typical slogan of dada. But here it lacked the divine afflatus that allowed Ball his supreme identification of the saint with the clown.

---

[37] Walter Mehring, *Berlin Dada* (Zurich: Verlag der Arche, 1959), 68–69.

John Heartfield, frontispiece from To Each His Own Football, 1919

The "death of art" was now greeted as a consequence of the advent of *Maschinenkunst*.

It was no longer a question of the "art of technological reproduction" but of the image of a "new world" in which the "revolt of the objects" — the dominating motif of bourgeois anguish — was tamed by the embrace between "liberated objects" and socialist man: exactly as in the finale of Mayakovsky's *Mystery-Bouffe*. The "light that comes from the East" was now an "electric message," as Yvan Goll wrote.[38] Soviet Russia, which in 1920 launched the Goelro plan for electrification and economic regionalization, was no longer the bearer of a reconciliatory ideology between man and nature, but rather an ideology that reconciled collectivity and technology. All of which could be accepted without objection by the Berlin dadaists. Had not the political program of Huelsenbeck and Hausmann recognized in the technological utopia the new, liberating ideology? In the face of such a prospect, dada's very spirit of contestation found itself in crisis. Or rather, the contestation now seemed a wholly contingent task, waiting to be able to create a productive organiza-

[38] In 1921, Yvan Goll wrote two fundamental articles "upon the death" of expressionism, which offer an eloquent testimony of the transformations undergone between 1921 and 1922 by the German movements whose aim was humanitarian revolution and cosmic pathos. "Expressionism," Goll wrote, "an amusement park of papier-mâché and stucco, with all its enchanted castles and human seraglios, is dismantled. The owner of the merry-go-round counts up his receipts. The revolutionary hangs himself behind the palisade. Soon, within an hour, nothing will remain but a heap of beams, dust, and rubbish. Expressionism is an old, abandoned barricade. The expressionist is a failed warmonger: too many stars have risen for peace." According to Goll, what expressionism lacked was *form* — as a result of which there was nothing to do but review all the *isms* to which the avant-garde gave life, precisely as Lissitzky and Arp would do. Yvan Goll, "Das Wort an sich," in *Die neue Rundschau*, II (1921), 1082 – 1085; see Paolo Chiarini, *Caos e geometria* (Florence: La Nuova Italia, 1969), 28 – 29. In a second article, Goll saw the old passwords ("Demand. Manifesto. Appeal. Accusation. Evocation. Ecstasy. Struggle. Man shouts. We are. One for the other. Pathos.") crushed by the civilization of the masses and the machine: sentimental pathos had given way to mechanical-cerebral strength. "New peoples step forward in the history of the world: the first word they address to us is electric." Y. Goll, "Der Expressionismus stirbt," in *Zenit*, no. 8 (1921), 8 ff. Cf. Chiarini, *Caos e geometria*, 29. A further phenomenon, parallel to the demise of expressionism, was the change brought about in 1919 in the dada movement by Arp, Baumann, Eggeling, Giacometti, Janco, and Richter, who founded the movement of dada radicals operating in Zurich until 1922 under the name "Das neue Leben" (see Marcel Janco, "Schöpferischer dada," in the volume *Dada, Monographie* ..., 45 ff.). The program of the new group called for participation "in the ideological evolution of the state," affirming that the spirit of abstract art implied an enormous extension of the human sense of freedom; the new objective was an art that was fraternal and clear in its abstractness, as well as openly interclassist. We have cited these examples in order to document a further aspect of the context of the European avant-gardes, upon which the activity of Lissitzky and van Doesburg were to be fundamental.

tion in the field of art and collective behavior, inspired in some way by the Soviet example.

In this climate, the arrival in 1920 of Ivan Puni and his wife Kseniya Boguslavskaya constituted for the Berlin avant-garde a kind of prelude to the philo-Soviet explosion that followed the arrival, one year later, of Ehrenburg, Lissitzky, and Gabo, and of the exhibition of Soviet art held in 1922 at the van Diemen Gallery on Unter den Linden.

While Kseniya was working for the Russian cabaret Karusell and for Juschny's Blaue Vogel, Puni organized in February 1921 his famous exhibition at the gallery Der Sturm, in which paintings and sheets of paper, clearly inspired by the geometry of Malevich and Lissitzky, were mounted in a deliberate disorder reminiscent of the antistructuralism of futurism. Enormous numbers and alphabet letters were superimposed on the paintings or allowed to show through between them, in an attempt to reaffirm the object quality of his work and to reconstruct the entire exhibition space as a "global object" (an obvious prelude to Lissitzky's *Prounenraum*, and a result of the experiments by Tatlin and Rodchenko on the tensions between formal objects and space).

The influences of dada were not lacking: on the occasion of the exhibition, Puni had men dressed in the style of Picasso's *Parade* going up and down the Kurfürstendamm. The total atmosphere created in the gallery thus overflowed into the street: Puni's "sandwich men" with their costumes inspired by Tatlin's *Counter-Reliefs*, by the *lettrismo* of Puni himself, by Ball's sacral clowning, by the marionette man of the Italian futurists, brought to life what remained crystallized in the galleries of Herwarth Walden. The pedagogical intent was no different from that of the provocative evenings of the negative avant-garde: what had changed, however, was its way of offering itself to the public, and not only because of the propagandist objectives of the paradoxical parade. In a certain way this latter challenged what went on in the exhibition galleries: it tried to raise "total ambiance" from its tomb.

Puni's work, furthermore, was anything but linear and coherent. Puni had signed the *Manifesto of Suprematism* on the occasion of the exhibition "0. 10," speaking of a liberation of the object from all meaning, of the destruction of its utilitarian aspect,[39] and at the same exhibition had collaborated with Male-

---

[39] See Herman Berninger and Jean-Albert Carter, *Pougny*, vol. I: *Les années d'avant-garde, Russie – Berlin, 1910 – 1923* (Tübingen: Ernst Wasmuth, 1972), 50 ff. and 153 – 158.

vich, Boguslavskaya, Klyun, and Menkov in a "collective painting." W. E. Groeger, in the catalogue of the exhibition at the Sturm, justified Puni's "naturalistic" works (circa 1919), considering them particular aspects of "artistic materialism"; but Puni himself, writing in *Iskusstvo Kommuny* in 1919, had affirmed:

> In order that the proletariat may be able truly to possess beautiful and useful objects, in order that beauty not be the attribute only of machines and plows, it is necessary to extend the utilitarian principle still further to the various branches of production.... And as for the artist ... what is left to him? Well, nothing but a sketch for a trademark — this little domain of "applied" art, which is his, will remain his.[40]

For Puni, there was a gap between art as a "creation of life" and pure art, which could never be bridged. His polemic was directed against orthodox productivity and represents a "rightist" interpretation of the same clash between form and production that would later be denounced by Tarabukin.[41]

In any event, this polemic was not grasped by Berlin culture. Puni's atelier — as Hans Richter also recalls[42] — became one of the most important centers of artistic encounters: Eggeling, Richter, Ehrenburg, Shklovsky, Hausmann, and Nell Walden met here periodically and wrote about it.

But Puni's arrival also gave rise to a chance encounter between German and Russian experiments; one has only to consider the finest painting that he did in Berlin, *The Musician* (1921), to judge the eccentricity of his experiments with respect to the constructivist current, which in 1922 catalyzed the Berlin intelligentsia. Other Russian eccentrics in Berlin at that time included Archipenko and Chaikov, as well as the group of Russian Jews who in 1922 published in Berlin the book *Rimon/milgrom* (Hebrew Artists in Contemporary Russian Art).

The exceptional concentration of Russian intellectuals in Berlin was in any event a highly significant phenomenon.

---

[40] Ibid., 167–168.
[41] See Nikolai Tarabukin, *Ot molberta k mashine* [From the Easel to the Machine] (Moscow: Proletkult, 1923), now in French translation, ed. Andrei B. Nakov, in the volume *Le dernier tableau: 1. Du Chevalet à la machine. 2. Pour une théorie de la peinture* (Paris: Editions Champ Libre, 1972). On the Puni room in the gallery Der Sturm, see also Germano Celant, *Ambiente-Arts. Dal futurismo alla Body Art* (Venice: La Biennale di Venezia, 1977), 20.
[42] See Hans Richter, "Begegnungen in Berlin," in *Avantgarde, Osteuropa 1910–1930* (Berlin, 1967), 13–21. On the Berlin art world, see also the catalogue *Paris–Berlin 1900–1933* (Paris: Musée d'Art Moderne de la Ville de Paris, 1978).

Ivan Puni, installation at the gallery Der Sturm, Berlin, 1921

Parade through the streets of Berlin on the occasion of Ivan Puni's exhibition, with costumes by Puni, 1921

Ivan Puni, The Musician, *1921*

One has to only think of the Russian club Haus der Künste, which gathered in the Café Leon. From 1922 to 1923 this was the meeting place of writers, artists, intellectuals, and poets such as Andrey Biely, Ilya Ehrenburg, Mayakovsky, Boris Pasternak, Igor Severyanin, Shklovsky, Elsa Triolet, Nikolai Berdyaev, S. Bulgakov, Natan Altman, Archipenko, Ivan and Kseniya Puni, Gabo, Lissitzky, David Shterenberg, Nikolai Zarecky, Osip Brik, and Roman Jakobson. It was clear that the Café Leon was the meeting place for the elite of the revolution who were disappointed by its initial results, agnostics, and intellectuals organically tied to Bolshevik power.

The concentration of Russian intellectuals in Berlin reached its apex precisely in 1922, the second year of the NEP, then suddenly diminished the following year, the year of the failed Communist attempt at insurrection and the beginnings of "German stabilization." Ehrenburg writes:

> I don't know how many Russians were living in Berlin in those years but there were clearly a great number of them, inasmuch as you could hear Russian spoken in every canton. Dozens of restaurants had been opened, complete with balalaikas, gypsies, blini, shashlik, and, of course, the inevitable Russian hysteria. A small variety theater was also operating. Three dailies and five weeklies were being published. In one year alone seventeen Russian publishing houses sprang up, putting out Fonvizin and Pilniak, cookbooks, treatises on patrology, technical manuals, memoirs, and pamphlets.[43]

It is Umansky who has related to us the occasion that brought both Kandinsky and Lissitzky to Berlin. The interest shown by the young artists of Berlin in the new Soviet artistic institutions in fact resulted in an invitation to Kandinsky to head the International Office of Russian Artists, with the task — which he never accomplished — of reconstructing the "Artistic International." In December 1921, Kandinsky thus arrived in Berlin, from there proceeding toward the Bauhaus at Weimar. Toward the end of 1921, Lissitzky received a similar assignment, and was permitted a surprising degree of freedom of movement given the unfavorable judgments expressed in Russia on his work. One can conclude that it was in the Soviet interest not to allow Russian culture in Berlin to remain the exclusive privilege of emigrants of

---

[43] Ilya Ehrenburg, *Uomini, anni, vita* (Rome: Edizioni Riuniti, 1972), 18; original ed. *Lyudi, gody, zhizn.*

the opposition and non-politicals; the exhibition of 1922, while still eclectic, clearly represents an attempt to regain control, officially, over ideological propaganda and contacts with the German intellectuals. These contacts were important for two reasons: for their propagandistic role and for the access to new levels of intervention to which they would lead.

It must not be forgotten that Soviet interest in Germany had a double aspect — political and technical. The revolutionary turmoil of November 1918 had been a blow to the Bolshevik party and, particularly after the deaths of Karl Liebknecht and Rosa Luxemburg, the relations between Russia and the KPD became intense. In 1923, the failed attempt to create a "German October" followed a plan of insurrection prepared in Moscow, to which Brandler and other leaders of the Communist party had been called.[44] It is clear that sending intellectuals in the guise of innocuous observers could be useful to Soviet Russia, but no proof exists that this was the political mandate of Lissitzky, Mayakovsky, or Ehrenburg. It is more probable that the primary motives here were those of ideological propaganda.

The second element of interest that Germany held for Soviet Russia was — as Lenin himself repeatedly emphasized[45] — its launching of a policy of economic planning, begun as a project of intensification and rationalization of military industries coordinated by Walther Rathenau and Moellendorff during the war. Furthermore, in 1920 the regional plan of the Ruhr covered a surface of 4500 square kilometers. For the Bolshevik party, which between 1920 and 1921 undertook its first experiment in planning, the German model served as a constant reference, even though all the Soviet theoreticians were careful to emphasize that there was much to criticize in this kind of capitalist system of planning. It remains a fact that, with the exhibition organized by

---

[44] See Ossip K. Flecktheim, *Il partito comunista tedesco (Kpd) nel periodo della Repubblica di Weimar* (Milan: Jaca Book, 1970), 198; orig. ed. *Die Kpd in der Weimarer Republik* (Offenbach, 1948; new ed., Frankfurt am Main, 1969).

[45] "History," Lenin wrote in the pamphlet *On the Tax on Nature* (1921), citing an article he wrote in 1918, "behaved in such a singular fashion that in 1918 it gave birth to socialist twins, separate from each other, which, like two future neophytes of a world socialist economy, found themselves in the same egg of international imperialism. Germany and Russia in the year 1918 achieved in the most distinct manner the material premises of the economic postulates of socialism — of the economy in general and of production in particular, on one side, and of the political conditions of socialism, on the other.... If birth of the revolution in Germany," he continues, "is delayed still further, it will be up to us *to learn* from the state capitalism of the Germans to use all forces to transplant it to our Soviet state, and not to overlook any dictatorial measure to hasten the adoption of this product of Western civilization on the part of barbarous Russia, nor to shrink from any barbarous methods in the struggle against barbarity."

El Lissitzky, sketch for the cover of the catalogue of the exhibition of Russian art at the van Diemen Gallery, Berlin, 1922

David Shterenberg at the van Diemen Gallery in 1922, the Berlin intellectual world was confronted with the *image of the ideology of the organization*. Apart from the works of the "rightist" current (Mashkov, Konchalovsky, Malyavin, Kustodiev), displayed in the lower hall of the gallery, the experiments of Lissitzky, Altman, Gabo, Pevsner, Rodchenko, Shterenberg, Mansurov, and the other suprematists and productivists, moved to the floor above, could be interpreted by their Berlin viewers as the bearers of a new technique of communication, above and beyond the usual divergences and debates existing among various currents and various artists.

The "wind from the East" had now assumed a concrete form for German intellectuals. The exhibition of 1922, with all its institutional importance, succeeded in presenting a common frame of reference within which comparison to the German experiments became inevitable.

Constructivism was a metaphor for the technical organization of the real, as we have already said. And in effect, from Lissitzky's *Prouny* to the experiments of the suprematists, to those of the youngest generations, which are documented by the production of the new schools of art, to the sculptures of Gabo, to the constructivist stage designs, the exhibition of 1922 throws into relief the original element of the Soviet avant-gardes: their tendency to a continuous, ideal form of design, seen as the dynamic articulation of signs that were completely disenchanted.[46]

The Berlin intellectuals thus found themselves violently confronted by an avant-garde that, with respect to the traditional current, arose as an answer — by turns desperate or cynical — to

[46] The 1922 exhibition at the van Diemen Gallery was organized by the official commissar David Shterenberg, with the collaboration of Marianov (Cheka), Natan Altman, Gabo, and Dr. Lutz, director of the gallery. Lissitzky, as Gabo has recently pointed out, had nothing to do with the organization of the exhibition; according to Gabo, even the cover of the catalogue, usually attributed to Lissitzky, was the work of Altman. See Naum Gabo, "The 1922 Soviet Exhibition," in *Studio International*, vol. CLXXXII, no. 938 (1971), 171. Shterenberg wrote the official text of the catalogue, and Arthur Holitscher the German text; the catalogue, edited in a hasty manner (as was, for that matter, the entire exhibition), contains many oversights and errors: Savyalov's *Construction in Relief* is credited to Tatlin, and Mansurov is spelled "Makurov," for example. See Shterenberg, *Russische Kunst in Berlin*, 19 – 20. The English translation of the texts of Shterenberg and Holitscher, and of the introduction to the catalogue *Erste russische Kunstausstellung, Berlin 1922*, is in the volume *The Tradition of Constructivism*, ed. Stephen Bann (New York: Viking, 1974), 70 – 76. On the 1922 exhibition, see also Andrei B. Nakov, "A Dialogue of the Deaf," in *Studio International*, vol. CLXXXVI, no. 960 (1973), 175 – 176. Among the negative reviews of the 1922 exhibition, notable is that contained in Paul Westheim's article, "Die Ausstellung der Russen," in *Das Kunstblatt*, 1922, 493 ff.

the tragic, and that now appeared under a new sign. Mayakovsky had lucidly forecast it in 1915:

> We consider the first part of our program of
> destruction to be concluded. And so do not be
> surprised if in our hands you no longer see the
> jester's rattle, but rather the architect's plan; do
> not be surprised if the voice of futurism, yester-
> day still soft with sentimental fancies, today rings
> out in the metal of sermons.[47]

The Soviet experiments, strong with the authority accorded them
by their having presented themselves as allies or protagonists of a
still-evolving socialism, demonstrated the absolute anachronism
not only of the populist and humanitarian appeals of the Arbeitsrat für Kunst, of the early Novembergruppe, or of the Sturm, but
also of the vitalistic and mystical didacticism of Itten's *Vorkurs*
and of the dadaist polemics. To be sure, the politicization of dada
was also linked, in Berlin, to the discovery of the "value of non-
value," of the technological utopia as a frame of reference for a
communication whose own specific space was that of the *Grossstadt* at the height of its anonymity, its perpetual and violent
metamorphosis, its presenting itself as a "theater of shock," of
the unforeseen, of the absurd. But it was still a discovery that
limited itself merely to specifying the instruments themselves — such as the technique of assemblage and of photomontage — without succeeding in indicating just how to put them to
institutional use. Between the graphic experiments of dada and
the compositions worked out by Lissitzky in Berlin — the illus-
trations for Ehrenburg's *Six Stories with Easy Endings*, published
by Helikon in 1929, those for Shklovsky's *Zoo*, the magazines
Veshch and *Broom*, the volume of the *Kunstismen*, the edition of
Mayakovsky's *Dlya Golossa*, etc. — the leap achieved was that
between a mere enunciation of principles and the systematic definition of a typographic language complete in itself.

The new dimension of the Soviet experiments was further confirmed by the exhibition, also in 1922, of the work of
Alexandra Exter at the Sarja bookstore on Marburgerstrasse, with
catalogue and text prepared by Jean Tugendkhold; by the show at
the same bookstore in 1923 of the work of Boguslavskaya and
Charchoune, and of the stage designs, miniature-scale models,
and costumes by Exter, Alexander Vesnin, Georg Stenberg, and

---

[47] Vladimir Mayakovsky, *Una goccia di fiele* [A Drop of Bile], published in the
almanac *Vzyal* [He seized] of December 1915; now in V. Mayakovsky, *Poesia e
rivoluzione* (Rome: Editori Riuniti, 1968), 74 – 77.

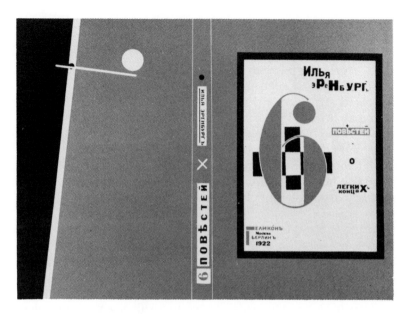

El Lissitzky, book jacket for Six Stories with Easy Endings *by Ilya Ehrenburg, Moscow — Berlin, 1922*

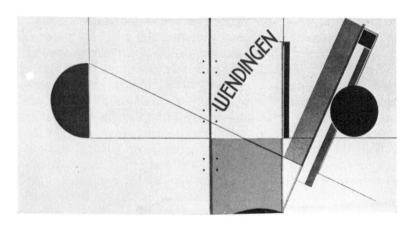

El Lissitzky, cover of the magazine Wendingen, *1923*

Georgii Yakulov on the occasion of the publication of Tairov's book *Das entfasselte Theater*, with graphics by Lissitzky; and finally by the appearance of the review *Veshch* (1922–1923).

The utopianism of the Glass Chain, of the ideal "cathedral of socialism," and of the *Stadtkrone*, suddenly appeared anachronistic: the publication of the review *Frühlicht*, edited by Bruno Taut — and containing an article by Iszelenov on Zholtovsky's naive scheme for a "socialist city," and one by Ehrenburg on the tower of Tatlin — can be seen as the final stage of an expressionist-dada "contamination" on the verge of extinction. The new dimension of international constructivism, immediately grasped by Moholy-Nagy and by Gropius, soon bore fruit. From 1922, Gropius and Adolf Meyer, with their projects for the Chicago Tribune Tower, the Kallenbach house, and the Kappe factory, appeared to be interpreting a *neue Sachlichkeit* far different from the preceding experiments.[48] In 1923 Gropius brought about a fundamental change in the didactics of the Bauhaus. Figures formerly absorbed in the general climate of expressionism, such as Mies van der Rohe and Hilberseimer, began to acquire far greater importance. Naturally, the reception accorded the Russian avant-garde was not unanimous. In *Das Kunstblatt*, Paul Westheim referred to the painters in the exhibition as "Oriental barbarians" — an expression already used against the Russians of the Blaue Reiter — recognizing, however, their intellectual affinity with the course leading to Malevich's *White on White* or Rodchenko's *Value of the Surface*.

At the same time, Waldemar George wrote four articles in the *Ere Nouvelle* extolling the theatrical activity of Tairov, of the constructivist directors, and of "leftist" tendencies in general, and calling for the show to be sent to Paris (a project later thwarted by the French government). In the liberal *Vossische Zeitung*, the critic Osborn singled out, instead, Konchalovsky and Falk as the major protagonists, together with Chagall and Filonov, of the "swinging to the left" of Soviet art, citing as its most prominent exponents Archipenko, Kandinsky, Shterenberg, and Altman, while remaining completely baffled by the works of the Unovis and of Tatlin. Among the more radical critics, however, mention should be made of Fritz Stahl, whose article in the *Berliner Tageblatt* we shall discuss shortly, and Andrey Biely, a theoretician and symbolist poet, from 1921 a follower of Rudolf Steiner and until 1912 professor of literature at the Proletkult, who called Lissitzky and Ehrenburg "specters of the antichrist."

[48] See Pehnt, *Gropius the Romantic*.

[49] Mention should also be made of the contrasts within tne Russian "colony" in

154

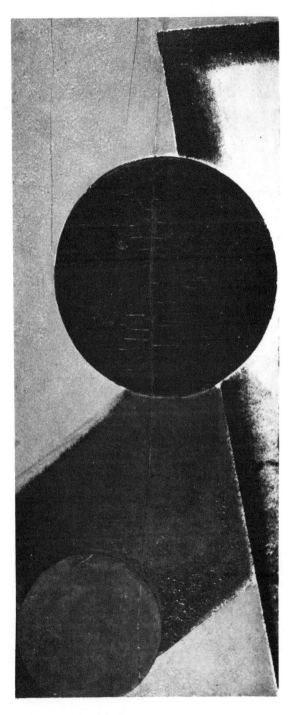

Alexander Rodchenko, Composition N73, *1918*

To these judgments must be added the evaluation of a representative of Hungarian constructivism such as Kállai with respect to Lissitzky's work — an opportunity Kállai himself used to clarify the new meanings that the contact with the Soviet avant-garde had hurled into the midst of parallel European tendencies.

Kállai wrote in 1921, "We have lost our unity with nature and the religion of the supernatural."[50] With these words he still seems to be echoing the anguished question concerning the destiny of the intellectual in the midst of a society whose disintegrating forces compromise his original "mandate," as set forth by Franz Marc in the almanac of the Blaue Reiter in 1912.[51]

But immediately afterward Kállai added:

Our paths run according to laws of energies dominated by science and technology, organized by reason. This can be regarded tragically or with satisfaction: for an art that does not want to remain a fiction, but that wants rather to bear up against the true facts of civilization, this situation creates the need to be moved not by subconscious and metaphysical impulses, but to be instead disciplined and intellectually clear in one's visual sensitivities. To spiritualize not organic growth, but abstract construction.

The man of the future, liberated from social anarchy and the dark ferment of psychosis ... is today still a beginning, a single cell, simple, elementary, but with definite possibilities of future historic realization. For this very reason, however, in no case must he become entangled in the net of the contradictory, impure relationships of the present, with its tattered and mediocre reality.[52]

For Kállai, then, the positiveness of the Lissitzkian object consisted of its intervention in a "space filled with energy," there being no doubt — as he himself would write in a second article on

Berlin. Ehrenburg speaks of the Café Leon as "a place similar to Noah's Ark, where the pure and the impure meet peacefully.... At a lecture given by the painter Puni," he continues, "the storm broke out; arguing furiously among themselves were Archipenko, Altman, Shklovsky, Mayakovsky, Shterenberg, Gabo, Lissitzky, and yours truly." Ehrenburg, *Uomini*, 20 – 21.

[50] Ernst Kállai, "Lisickij," in *Das Kunstblatt*, VI, no. 1 (1921).

[51] See Franz Marc, I *"Fauves" tedeschi* (Bari, 1967), 24 – 28; original ed. "Die 'Wilden' Deutschlands," in *Der Blaue Reiter* (Munich, 1912), 5 – 7.

[52] Kállai, "Lisickij."

the Soviet artist, which appeared in *Der Cicerone*[53] — that that object was nothing but a fictional construction of a fictional mechanism.

But it was precisely this "fiction" that shook the German artistic world. It was this explicit ideological function that was characteristic of a perspective that — in order to be expressed with all the fullness and completeness that belong to pure intellectual elaboration — had to remain just that: a horizon constantly shifted forward, in order to catalyze Berlin artistic circles by impressing upon them a decisive development, and contributing, moreover, to their unification.

But it was also this basis for the reunification of avant-garde ideology — a primary objective of Lissitzky, quite evident in the publication of the *Kunstismen* — that could not receive official party approval in Russia. Anatolii Lunacharsky personally undertook to review the Berlin exhibition of 1922, paying particular attention to the reactions of the German critics. And it is significant that Lunacharsky's sympathies were with the most critical of the German reviewers, Stahl: that is to say, with an avowed anti-Soviet, who even compared the U.S.S.R. to the Germany of Kaiser Wilhelm. Lunacharsky nevertheless was willing to overlook such "liberal stupidities," as he called Stahl's polemical barbs at the Soviet regime, in order to be able to cite certain remarks made by the German critic that could possibly assume a different meaning in the context of his own cultural politics. Stahl wrote in a passage cited *in toto* by Lunacharsky:

> If the old represented merely a tendency parallel to that of the West, little different from the art of the academy, in leftist art cerebral acrobatics reigned supreme, a phase that we in Germany have already passed through.... There is no doubt that a particular harmony exists between the revolutionary art of these painters and the revolutionary character of the Soviet power itself. This power, in fact, wants to create new and extraordinary forms by destroying everything old, but in painting this revolutionary spirit is expressed in completely abstract forms, which go to extremes and end up as simply absurd, forms that the people are not likely to accept.[54]

[53] Kállai, "El Lisickij," in *Der Cicerone*, XVI, no. 2 (1924), 1058–1063.

[54] Anatolii Lunacharsky, "L'esposizione russa a Berlino," in *Rassegna sovietica*, no. 1 (1965), 110–116; original ed. in *Izvestia*, no. 273 (1922). In order to understand the reasons for Lunacharsky's attitude toward the avant-garde intellectuals and

It was precisely these final remarks that won Lunacharsky's approval. He emphasized the populist tones of Stahl's arguments, taking up again a polemic dear to the Proletkult. Stahl had written, "It would be better to teach the people technologies and trades exclusively, leaving it to them to define their own new style" — a concept too close, for various reasons, to both the cultural politics proclaimed by Lenin and to Trotsky's observations on the task of "productive" art not to have been taken up again by Lunacharsky. In fact, Lunacharsky wrote:

> Stahl states peremptorily that, once freed from the exterior influence of the intellectual groups, the people would return to their own resources — their warmth of feeling, richness of fantasy, musical refinement, use of colors, etc.

> I hasten to declare that on many points my judgment coincides with that of the bourgeois critic. There was no doubt that our pseudo-progressive aspiration to exclude feeling and fantasy from art, to intellectualize it at all costs, is not counterbalanced by the enfeebled, lax forms of our academic and semi-academic past. I too believe that the new generation now being educated in our schools is capable of mirroring the revolution in forms far richer and more immediate than those employed by leftist extremists, excellent men all, and often sincerely friends of the revolution, but nonetheless influenced by the bourgeois leftist art of the Parisian *bohème*.[55]

If up to this point the attitude of the People's Commissar for Artistic Instruction appears to have been extremely cautious, careful to balance criticism of an anti-academic nature with that directed at the avant-garde tradition, in the succeeding passage his discourse assumed a decidedly Trotskyist tone:

> Our exhibition in Berlin did not fully reflect either the today or, in particular, the tomorrow of our art. It reflected only those conjunctural peculiarities in the midst of which we have lived these past years, that is, the influx of forces from the

the role he assigned to the organization of culture, a fundamental work is Sheila Fitzpatrick's *The Commissariat of Enlightenment. Soviet Organisation of Education and the Arts under Lunacharsky, October 1917 – 1921* (Cambridge: Cambridge Univ. Press, 1970). See also Giovanna Spendel, *Gli intellettuali sovietici negli anni '20* (Rome, 1979), for the political-literary debate carried on in the Soviet cultural journals that were more or less directly linked to party organizations.

[55] Lunacharsky, *L'esposizione*.

leftist front of prerevolutionary art. Nonetheless,
it is pleasing to observe that even an exhibition of
works born of this transitional phase has elicited
from both the German critics and public such a
favorable reception ...

An art in transition, the direct heir of the avant-gardes, of the
prerevolutionary progressivist bourgeoisie: Lunacharsky's
"official" judgment can be immediately compared to Trotsky's
considerations on just this "transitional" role specific to the
Soviet artistic avant-gardes.[56]

Before drawing a conclusion from Lunacharsky's review,
it is necessary to compare it to an article that in a way constituted
a reply to it, formulated explicitly by the "leftist artistic front." In
1923 Mayakovsky, in *Krasnaya nov*, deemed it necessary to reply,
on a specifically political level, to the People's Commissar.[57]

Mayakovsky too lamented the incompleteness of the Berlin exhibition, but he avoided using this factor to further other
ends, as Lunacharsky had done. What interested him was rather
to emphasize immediately that what he calls "the revolutionary
exhibition" was inaugurated on the very day on which in the
streets of Berlin, near the Busch Circus, the German Communists
skirmished with the Nationalists. "This fact," he continued,
"influenced the revolutionary mood, and the exhibition was
inaugurated in an atmosphere of good feeling."[58]

Mayakovsky did not point to this coincidence gratui-
tously. He viewed the exhibition at the van Diemen Gallery as
being under the "moral" sign of avant-garde art: the lower floor,
dedicated to "right-wing painting," appears in his article as
merely a useful element for the correct evaluation of the
"left-wing art" gathered in the upper hall. There was a connection between the uprisings organized by the KPD and the success
of the first exhibition of Soviet art; Mayakovsky's objective was to
demonstrate the propaganda value of the avant-garde experiments, and in a truly political sense.[59] He wrote:

[56] See Leon Trotsky, *Literature and Revolution* (Ann Arbor: Univ. of Michigan
Press, 1960).
[57] V. Mayakovsky, "La mostra di arte figurativa della Rsfr a Berlino," in *Rassegna
sovietica*, no. 1 (1965), 108 – 109; original ed. in *Krasnaya nov*, no. 2 (1923).
[58] Ibid.
[59] Mayakovsky went so far as to identify conservative tendencies with the political and counterrevolutionary right: "The conservatives," he wrote, "arriving in a
foreign country, often allow themselves to be enticed by the plate of lentils of the
American millionaires, and try to make themselves agreeable by making insinua-
tions regarding the new regime. This type of trick was pulled by the noted painter
Malyavin, for example. Treated with kid gloves in Russia, sent abroad with our
consent and assistance, he then proceeded to grant an interview to the white 'rag'

It is evidently impossible to judge from this exhibition what is happening in Russia. Our main force lies not in the paintings, good as they may be, but rather in a new organization of art, particularly in the schools, in industry, and in the union movement, which imparts to our art a new vital force, unknown in Europe. It is essential to demonstrate by every means possible this particular aspect of the work being done in the Soviet Union.

Europe is trying to move away from us politically, but is unable to stop the growing interest in Russia, and thus is trying to find another outlet by opening up the safety valve of art. France, for example, which is so reluctant to grant a visa to an individual Soviet citizen, grants it to the Theater of Art, and it would scarcely have been a surprise if Millerand's wife herself took over the leadership of the Committee to boost our exhibition in Paris. We must make certain that as many communist ideas as possible filter through this aperture.

Thus the identification of communism with the avant-garde was again strengthened by Mayakovsky. A Soviet art exhibition in a capitalist country was for him a vehicle of ideological penetration, provided that it was shaped by constructivist currents. The clash between Lunacharsky and Mayakovsky becomes more comprehensible in this light. For the People's Commissar — politically pressed by Lenin's criticisms — the "left-wing" factions already revealed values that were all potentially assimilable by the evolving capitalist universe — exactly as Tugendkhold would note three years later in reviewing the 1925 Paris Exposition.[60] For Lunacharsky, the only possible course was that of a return to the great themes of bourgeois humanism; it was the "solution" that

Rul, an interview of recrimination against Soviet Russia, where — are you listening? — they prevented him from working" (ibid.). It is evident that the incident provoked by Malyavin — who was later to steal his own paintings and hand them over to the speculator Kogan to send to the United States — and the letter sent to the same _Rul_ by Sinezubov (another "right-wing" painter) were used by Mayakovsky to try to break down the ever more cautious official line of the Commissariat for Public Instruction regarding avant-garde tendencies. "The Americans," Mayakovsky continued, "acquire the sculptures, paintings, and samples of applied art of these [right-wing] artists. The newspapers assert that they are the ones who will give birth to the pictorial art of the future Russia."

[60] See J. Tugendkhold, "Stile 1925," in _Rassegna sovietica_, no. 3 (1967), 107–109; original ed. "Stil 1925," in _Pechat' i revolyutsiya_, 1925.

Lukács and, in architecture, the Vopra group were to offer to the ideology of "socialist art."

For Mayakovsky, as for Rodchenko, Arvatov, or Brik, there existed only one consumer "who doesn't know what to do with paintings, nor with ornaments, and who does not fear iron and steel," and "this consumer is the proletariat."[61] This thesis in itself needs no comment, but its appeal takes on a particular value with regard to the diverse meaning assumed by the Berlin exhibition for a responsible party member and for the avant-garde intellectuals.

The truth is that Mayakovsky considered himself, just as did Lissitzky for the figurative arts, the "official envoy of the opposition" in the West. In the name of the "social mandate" that they claimed for themselves, both believed themselves able to enter into a direct dialectic with the Party; thus it may well be that their ideological propaganda in the West had as a second purpose the strengthening of the position of the intellectual avant-gardes within Soviet Russia, as a result of the prestige received from the acclamation of the European intellegentsia.

It thus becomes essential to follow closely the cultural politics conducted in Germany by the principal propagandist of constructivist ideological themes, Lissitzky.

It is in fact extremely significant that Lissitzky, while discussing on diverse occasions the Berlin artistic atmosphere, felt it necessary to attack both the Sturm group and the politicized dadaist group.

In the first number of *Veshch*, he insisted on an international perspective identified with the objectivity of constructivism:

> From now on, art, while preserving all local characteristics and symptoms, is international. The founders of a new guild of painters are making sure that the links are securely established between Russia, which experienced the most powerful revolution, and the West, with its miserable, postwar Black Monday mood; in doing this, they are ignoring all distinctions between psychological, economic, and purely national art. "Object" provides the link between two adjacent lines of communication.[62]

And he continued, echoing the words of Mayakovsky in 1915:

[61] Osip Brik, "Into Production!" in *Lef*, no. 1 (1923).
[62] El Lissitzky, "The Blockade of Russia Moves toward Its End," in *Veshch*, no. 1–2 (1922).

We consider the negative tactic of the "dadaists," who are as similar to the early futurists of the prewar era as one pea is to another, to be anachronistic. The time has come to build on open ground. Whatever is exhausted will die anyway, without assistance from us; for land that is lying fallow needs not a program, not a school of thought, but simply work.[63]

In the third number of *Veshch* the attack was directed at late expressionism, as well as at the sculpture of Archipenko and the painting of Kandinsky, the former criticized for its "saccharine quality," and the latter for its "lack of clarity and compactness," for its extraneousness to the *object*. Lissitzky was basically concerned with liquidating the last late-romantic ferments, underlining the escapism of the experiments of the Russian artists who had deliberately cut themselves off from the political debate of the avant-gardes. He wrote:

> One expects to find modern art at the Galerie Der Sturm; but this giant ocean liner has changed into a shabby little tramp. A short time ago the Hungarians could be seen there. Begotten of the Revolution in Russia, along with us they have become productive in their art. Moholy-Nagy has prevailed over German expressionism, and is striving to achieve an organized approach. Against the background of the jellyfish-like nonobjective painting, the clear geometry of Moholy and Peri stands out in relief....
>
> The culture of painting no longer comes from the museum. It comes from the picture gallery of our modern streets — the riot and exaggeration of colors on the lithographic poster, the black glass signs with white letters pasted on, the light from electric lamps that have been colored with violet lacquer.[64]

---

[63] Ibid.

[64] El Lissitzky, "Exhibitions in Berlin," in *Veshch*, no. 3 (1923). Compare this article with the other one published in *Veshch* (no. 1–2, 1922), under the pseudonym of Ulen, "Die Ausstellungen in Russland," 18–19, in which he points out the significance of the exhibition of the Obmoku group in Moscow (1921), as well as that of the Unovis group. It is interesting to recall Ehrenburg's opinion, even more negative than Lissitzky's, on Berlin expressionism of the twenties: "I visited several exhibitions of the Sturm, and beheld not paintings, not art, but rather the hysteria of those who, instead of pistols or bombs, had taken up paintbrushes or tubes of paint"(Ehrenburg, *Uomini*, 11). Furthermore, the most politicized expressionist circles after 1921 claimed that they had lost all faith in the Russia of

The pictorial culture that "comes from the gallery of our modern streets" was, in sum, the program of the non-verbal techniques of communication that the entire avant-garde had turned to, from Meidner's manifesto on the big city, to the "factograph" championed later by Lef. But it was also, and principally, the justification of the technique of montage, championed by Hausmann (with the approval, it seems, of Lissitzky himself) as a specific innovation of the Berlin dada, but brought to the highest linguistic level by Kurt Schwitters.[65]

And, in fact, it was with Schwitters that Lissitzky set up an organic collaborative relationship. Through Schwitters, he came into contact with the Kestner Society of Hanover, and with his help, as well as that of others, later succeeded in entering a Swiss sanitorium. Lissitzky and Schwitters together edited numbers seven and eight of *Merz*, the "Merz-Nasci," and, together with Hans Richter and Mies van der Rohe, created the elementarist review *G*. This collaboration poses a historical problem — the same posed by Lissitzky's collaboration with Arp, with whom he edited the *Kunstismen*, or with van Doesburg — as to the precise choice made by the Soviet artist in the composite panorama of the European avant-gardes.

In number two of *Merz* (1923), Schwitters, together with Arp, van Doesburg, Christoph Spengemann, and Tzara, signed the *Manifest Proletkunst*, explicitly directed against "political" art — an attack that had been preceded in 1921 by his article "Merz" in *Der Ararat:*[66]

> Art is a spiritual function of man, and its object is to free him from the chaos of life (from its tragedy). Art is free in the use of its own means, but is subject to its own internal laws.... Trivial as it may sound, no real difference exists between

the NEP; Ehrenburg himself (p. 15) cites in this regard the poets of the group Die Aktion and the collaborators of the Rote Fahne.

[65] On the theme, which is really rather pointless, of the *invention* of the photomontage, see, among others, Hausmann, *Courrier Dada;* Richter, *Dada;* Scharf, *John Heartfield;* Steneberg, *Russische Kunst in Berlin* (the chapter "Film Foto Montage"); Dawn Ades, *Photomontage: Photography as Propaganda* (London: Thames and Hudson, 1976), an extremely informative work, with an ample bibliography. Interesting as a historical document is Louis Aragon's article, "John Heartfield et la beauté révolutionnaire," in *Commune*, no. 21 (1935), 985 – 991, in which, having made a clear distinction between cubist collage and dadaist collage, Aragon presents surrealism as an attempt to synthesize humanism and dada negation. Furthermore, he draws a parallel between Heartfield's collage and Rimbaud's *Saison en Enfer.*

[66] Kurt Schwitters, "Merz," in *Der Ararat*, II, no. 1 (1921), 3 – 9, in which Huelsenbeck's position (which Schwitters calls that of the "husk Dada") is harshly attacked.

paintings showing the imperial army led by Napoleon and the Red Army led by Trotsky.... The art that we want is neither proletarian nor bourgeois, inasmuch as it undertakes to influence culture in its structure, without letting itself be influenced in turn by social conditions.[67]

If the first phrase quoted was largely influenced by the manifestos of de Stijl and by the theories of Mondrian, filtered through van Doesburg — art as a liberation from suffering — the second part of the quotation is similar in every detail to the theses of the Russian formalists, and in particular to those of Shklovsky and Tretyakov, where these two affirm that ideology "does not lie in the material that art makes use of, but rather in the procedures of working out this material,[68] and that art "is not a thing ... but a relationship of materials, and, like every relationship, it is of zero degree ... [hence] happy works, tragic works, universal works, or chamber works, *the contrasts of one world to another or of a cat to a stone are equal.*"[69]

Schwitters thus resolutely denied the utopia of a "political" art in favor of a production of formal objects conceived as a pure clash of neutral signs — even if they were extracted from unused vestiges of everyday life. In this sense, the alliance formed by Lissitzky and Schwitters becomes even more significant: it was not so much the "artistic left" that interested Lissitzky, but the author of "Merz," who from the beginning had been driven away from the Berlin dada group by the activities of Huelsenbeck.[70] And besides, even Moholy-Nagy — who did not enjoy the sympathies of Lissitzky for "technical reasons" — had written for the review *MA* in 1922 an article entitled *Konstruktivis-*

---

[67] See the "Manifest Proletkunst," in *Merz*, no. 2 (1923), 24 – 25 (now in *Almanacco Dada*, 481). See also in the same number of *Merz* Kurt Schwitters's article "War." In *Merz*, no. 1 (1923), 7 – 8, Schwitters wrote, "We hope that our activity, the purpose of which is to show the enormous lack of style of our culture, will arouse a strong desire and a great nostalgia for style. Then our most important activity will begin. We will turn against dada and will fight further only for style.... Style is the result of collective work." On Schwitters's approach to abstract elementarism, starting from the poetic experiments of August Stamm and from Herwarth Walden's *Wortkunsttheorie*, up to his contacts with van Doesburg, see Forte, *La poesia*, 104 – 118 (the chapter "Merz-Schwitters: universo 'irrelato' e ipotesi manierista").

[68] Sergey Tretyakov, "Buon anno, buon 'nuovo Lef,'" in Giorgio Kraiski, *Le poetiche russe del '900* (Bari, 1968), 238 – 242; original ed. "S novym godom, S novym Levom," in *Novyi lef*, no. 1 (1928). On the history of the reviews directed by Mayakovsky, from *Iskusstvo kommuny* to *Novyi lef*, see *L'arte dopo la rivoluzione*, ed. Luigi Magarotto (Rome, 1976).

[69] Viktor Shklovsky, *Rozanov* (Petrograd, 1921), 4. My italics.

[70] On the conflicts between Schwitters and Huelsenbeck, see, among others, Werner Schmalenbach, *Kurt Schwitters* (Cologne: DuMont Schauberg, 1967).

Natan Altman, Collage, *1923*

Laszlo Moholy-Nagy, Dada-Collage, *1920*

mus und das Proletariat, in which were set forth highly ambiguous theses on the internationalism of constructivism. In Moholy-Nagy's article, in effect, the spirit of the machine was shown to be *in itself* the bearer of social egalitarianism, but only insofar as "everyone can become masters or slaves" of the machine itself. The "root of socialism," in the words of Moholy-Nagy himself, was in the objectivity and collectivism imposed by the new technologies. Moholy-Nagy essentially was picking up the demands championed by the abstract cinema of Eggeling, by the metropolitan thematic that had been present in German culture from the beginning of the century, or by the forces that tended toward a synthesis of the avant-gardes. His screenplay *Dynamik der Grossstadt* tended to make of montage a technique directly inspired by a reading of the metropolitan universe, and it is perhaps no accident that a passage of his "Malerei, Photographie, Film" of 1925 is but a paraphrase of Simmel's famous text on the metropolis and nervous life.[71] The need to give unity to the kaleidoscope of the avant-gardes is further evidenced by the *Buch neuer Künstler*, which Moholy-Nagy published in 1922 with Lajos Kassák, while, as we shall see later, in 1921 Moholy-Nagy was close to Hausmann, Puni, and Arp. If from a technical point of view the work of Moholy-Nagy thus shows a consequentiality of its own, it is only right to recognize the extreme ambiguity of his political position. To be sure, socialism is "mentioned" in the article *Konstruktivismus und das Proletariat* (always assuming that the article is not apocryphal); but the phrase "there is no tradition in technology, there is no consciousness of class or rank" should be cause for reflection. One might observe, first of all, that the immediate identification of technological impersonality with socialism is so naive (or cynical) as to be considered a symptom that in itself should be historicized. Undoubtedly, the political uncertainty of the review *MA* also affected Moholy-Nagy after 1922. Kemény and Moholy-Nagy, together with Kállai and Laszlo Peri, signed a declaration in favor of the Proletkult,[72]

---

[71] Moholy-Nagy wrote, "With the enormous development of technics and large cities, our organs of perception have increased their capacity to carry on optical and acoustical functions simultaneously.... Berliners cross Potsdamer Platz; they speak, and at the same time they listen: automobile horns, streetcar bells, the horns of the bus, the cabman's shout, the noise of the subway, the newsboys' cries, the sounds issuing from a loudspeaker, etc., and they can distinguish all these acoustical stimuli. A poor provincial, on the other hand, finding himself by chance in the same square, is so shaken by the great number of impressions received that he stops frozen in his tracks in front of an oncoming streetcar." L. Moholy-Nagy, "Pittura, fotografia, film," in Gianni Rondolino, *László Moholy-Nagy: pittura, fotografia, film* (Turin, 1975), 110; original ed. "Malerei, Photographie, Film," in *Bauhausbücher*, no. 8 (Munich: A. Langen, 1927), 41.

without realizing that they were thus supporting an organization totally antithetical to their experiments; but in 1924 they advocated in *Der Sturm* an art composed of a "system of dynamo-constructive forms," accentuating the material "only as a conveyor of energies."[73]

All things considered, it is pointless to follow the intellectual peregrinations of the artists converging on Berlin and in search of political roots solely to obtain justifications for their experiments. It may be observed, however, that in the alleged "socialism" of Moholy-Nagy there lay not only the technological utopia expressed at its maximum level by Benjamin in his *The Work of Art in the Age of Mechanical Reproduction*, but also the heritage of Kautsky's Social Democracy: the machine — like the great trust that subjugates it — was a prime requisite of social transformation. To spread the word regarding its functioning, as Moholy-Nagy, Hans Richter, or Lissitzky did, was not contradictory to plunging it — while dominating it, "holding it together" — into the sea of the topsy-turvy alphabets of the metropolis, as Hausmann or Schwitters did. It was rather a matter of an interiorization or of an exteriorization of the impulses generated by the "new Babylon." Van Doesburg would demonstrate, completely absorbing the subjective alienation provoked by it, that dada could take on an experimental guise, and elementarism the technique of collage.

All this does no more than document the decline (temporary — think of the virtually contemporary formation of the surrealist group) of the late-expressionist and dada "revolutionary" inclinations.

With Schwitters, and with the catalyzing influences of the 1922 show, of *Veshch*, of *G*, of the "turning point" in the Bauhaus after 1923, of the formation, in essence, of a "Constructivist International," the technical pole of avant-garde work became separated from the encrustations of content that had been superimposed on it. The ideology of permanent innovation (the *shock technique*) was now looked upon as the principal instrument of an out-and-out "theory of the sign," directed solely at controlling the unsettling tensions created between society and a technological universe in rapid transformation.

But it is also interesting in this regard to recall the testi-

---

[72] See "Nyilatkozat," in *Egység*, no. 4 (1923), 16. On the early years of Moholy-Nagy's artistic activity, see, in addition to Rondolino, *László Moholy-Nagy*, the essay by Krisztina Passuth, "Debut of László Moholy-Nagy," in *Acta Historiae Artium*, XIX, no. 1−2 (1973), 125−142.

[73] L. Moholy-Nagy and Alfred Kemény, "Dynamisch-konstruktivistisches Kraftsystem," in *Sturm*, no. 12 (1922), 186.

mony of a "pure" intellectual such as Erich Bucholz, who offers a symptomatic picture of the discussions within the Western constructivist group. Bucholz himself affirmed that in 1922, together with Peri, he had singled out architecture as a point of arrival for the avant-garde. Even more significant discussions, inasmuch as they came from the Hungarian group in Berlin, were those of Kállai, Kemény, and Huszar:

> Theme of the debate: dynamics; the model: Tatlin and the futurists. The central theme of the discussion was familiar. Transported into kinetics, we tested it out, together with Eggeling. I maintained the opinion that within the sphere of painting, statics and dynamics did not constitute isolated values, in absolute opposition to each other, nor were they antithetical principles, even less so if considered in terms of chromatic relationships. In terms of the formal equation *Constructivism Equals Dynamics of the Revolution*, dynamics, taken by itself, constituted an abuse, and Kállai countered me: "Think of electricity and you will know what dynamics is."[74]

Essentially, then, beyond the discussion on the symbolic value of constructivism, the true theme of the debate was the possible cognitive value of artistic elementarism. Bucholz wrote further:

> We persisted above all in discussing two opposing conceptions of the term "conscious." If the circle and the line were the instruments that constituted the point of departure, the essential requisites; in light of the affinity of our work, the question was understandably posed: "What was the process of construction?" Here our opinions became tangled. My reply was that our creations had to spring from an irresistible impulse, governed by an eye that measured and thought with but one goal: the final result. The work was thus "that which has been rendered conscious." Lissitzky answered me sarcastically: "Romantic."[75]

After all, Bucholz was not alone in his attempt to transport the last vestiges of expressionist pathos into the elementarist language. Think of Moholy-Nagy's work between 1920 and 1921,

[74] Erich Bucholz, "Begegnung mit osteuropäischen Künstlern," in *Avantgarde Osteuropa*, 26.
[75] Ibid.

or of Puni himself. Even here Lissitzky's opposition was symptomatic and clearly reveals his cultural politics. A cultural politics, in any event, that began to reveal its internal ambiguities with the publication of the review *Veshch/Gegenstand/Objet*, which he directed together with Ehrenburg, as mentioned above, from 1922. *Veshch's* program was explicit. Objective art, the metaphor of the technological universe in dynamic growth, and the image of a mechanized production capable of pacifying the collectivity in an organic plan were here greeted as concrete moments of common work of the *Constructivist International*. In this sense, *Veshch* was a political act: the ideology of the plan emerged as a unifying moment of the Soviet intellegentsia and of that of the West as well.

> *Veshch*
> will champion a constructive art, whose mission is not, after all, to embellish life but to organize it.
> We have named our review
> *Veshch*
> because to us art means nothing other than the creation of new "objects."...
> Every organized piece of work — whether it be a house, a poem, a painting — is a practical "object," not intended to estrange people from life.... Thus we have nothing in common with those poets who announce in verse that they will not write any more verse, or painters who use the picture as a means of publicizing their renunciation of painting. Basic utilitarianism is far from our thoughts.[76]

Compare this programmatic passage with the very premises of the review:

> The blockade of Russia moves toward its end. The appearance of *Veshch* is an indication of the fact that the exchange of "objects" between young Russian and West European masters has begun.
> We are standing in the dawn of a great creative era.... The days of destroying and beleaguering and undermining are behind us....
> We consider the triumph of the construc-

---

[76] From *Veshch*, no. 1 − 2 (1922), programmatic platform. On *Veshch's* position with relation to Lef and to the political climate of the NEP, see Giorgio Kraiski's "Lef contre Nep," in *VH 101*, no. 7 − 8 (1972), 157 − 164, even though the author's conclusions are, in my opinion, highly debatable.

tive method to be essential for our present. We find it not only in the new economy and in the development of industry, but also in the psychology of our contemporaries in art.[77]

The theme of dissent from the dadaist positions was thus reaffirmed. The impossible politicization of a falsely destructive ideology was grasped in an explicit manner. But asserted at the same time was the need for intellectual work that stopped at the doors of industrial production, that touched the world of labor only tangentially, that did not abandon the field of pure ideology. And it was on the slippery terrain of ideology that *Veshch* presumed to follow the Leninist directions on Russia's overtures toward a Europe experimenting with advanced techniques of state capitalism. (The reference to the NEP in the programmatic platform of *Veshch* is significant.)

The ideological ambiguity of the operation was accentuated by the contemporary writings of Ehrenburg, and in particular by his volume *And Yet It Moves!*, also of 1922, in which one notes the emergence of the red thread that joins together movements such as the Esprit Nouveau, de Stijl, Unovis, and the Vida Americana under the banner of an internationalism with a constructivist line. With a warning, however:

> An art constructed in the proper way can exist only in the midst of a society that is organized in a rational manner....
>
> Can a cubist who constructs his painting according to a rigorous equilibrium of forms and an impeccable interdependence of weight among the various colors breathe freely in a state founded on chance, the arbitrary, and anarchic confusion?... Can an artist who finds his pathos in creating an object, in transforming material, bestow his approval on contemporary Europe, which prefers not to produce but rather to quarrel over the destruction of what has already been produced?
>
> The new art favors a single plan, a system, an organization, in contrast with the anarchic impressionism of petit-bourgeois society ...[78]

Art thus emerged as an image of the ideology of *Rationalisierung*

---

[77] *Veshch*, no. 1–2 (1922).

[78] I. Ehrenburg, *And Yet It Moves* (Moscow–Berlin, 1922).

Fernand Léger, drawings for And Yet It Moves! *by Ilya Ehrenburg,
Moscow — Berlin, 1922*

upheld as an eminently socialist value; the anarchy of distribution and productive passivity were designated, on the other hand, as the non-values of the capitalist bourgeoisie.

To this distorted interpretation of the reality of international capitalism, then in the process of reorganization, Ehrenburg added a new slogan: the rationalist tendencies of intellectual ideology were to him — as they were to Lissitzky — the substantial new forms "of opposition" in the Western countries. Hence, the legitimacy of the Constructivist International.

Immediately Boris Arvatov accused *Veshch* of opportunism in the pages of *Pechat' i revolyutsiya*.[79] For Arvatov, the union of forces that had gathered around the review — Archipenko, Chaplin, Craig, Gleizes, Goll, Léger, Jules Romains, Severini, etc. — was only a concentration of aestheticizing intellectuals in their first contact with the productive universe, around the new fetish of modern technique seen not as a means but as an end. Between Lunacharsky's criticism of the 1922 show and that of Arvatov directed at *Veshch*, there lay at least an area of mutual agreement. The technological universe, evoked outside of a recovery of the *city of man*, too clearly carried for them the mark of "objectivity" to be accepted in itself as a valid ideology of support for the universe of "socialist work."

Yet it was this very technological utopia, intent on identifying aesthetics with the ideology of production, that was singled out by Ehrenburg and Lissitzky as a catalyst for the dispersed European efforts.

All of which was already clear in Lissitzky's manifesto "Proun" (1920), made known in Europe by van Doesburg's review in 1922:

> Proun is the name we give to the stage on the way to neoplasticism, which is rising on the ground fertilized by the dead bodies of pictures and their painters. The pictures crashed together with the church and its god, whom it served as a proclamation; with the palace and its king, whom it served as a throne; with the sofa and its philistine, whose icon of happiness it was....
>
> We have set the Proun in motion and so we obtain a number of axes of projection; we

[79] Boris I. Arvatov, "Critique of Veshch," in *Pechat' i revolyutsiya*, no. 7 (1922). On the *Veshch* affair, see also K. Volodin's article, "La rivista Vesč'" in *Rassegna sovietica*, no. 2 (1969), 264–268; original ed. "Zhurnal Veshch," in *Dekorativnoe iskusstvo*, no. 5 (1968). See also Kestutis Paul Zygas, "The Magazine Veshch-Gegenstand-Objet," in *Oppositions* 5 (1976), 113–128.

stand between them and push them apart. Standing on this scaffolding in the space we must begin to mark it out. Emptiness, chaos, the unnatural, become space, that is: order, certainty, plastic form, when we introduce markers of a specific kind and in a specific relationship to each other. The structure and the scale of the group of markers give the space a specific tension. By changing the markers we alter the tension of the space, which is formed from one and the same emptiness....
Proun's power is to create aims. This is the artist's freedom, denied to the scientist.
Purpose results in usefulness, which means the depth of quality is spread into the breadth of quantity.[80]

Apart from the specific linguistic instruments used, it is clear that notable affinities exist between the Lissitzkian Proun and the ideas of the de Stijl group; it may, in fact, be said that if constructivism appeared almost totally new to Berlin, the avant-gardes gathered around the "Stijl" had for some time been following the program with which Lissitzky proposed to reunify the European experiments. As in the case of Schwitters, here too, unexpressed but implicit, was the political aspiration of Russian constructivism. The Lissitzky-van Doesburg alliance itself was based on an acceptance of an avant-garde in which the "revolutionary" wills

[80] El Lissitzky, "Proun," in *De Stijl*, V, no. 6 (1922), 81–85. In considering Lissitzky's work of the early 1920s, it is, however, necessary to keep in mind his ties with Jewish culture and the mysticism that he consequently attributes to signs and to letters of the alphabet. In this regard, Birnholz emphasizes the ties between Lissitzky's culture and Malevich's, considering *Proun 99* as the culmination of a search for a dematerialization of geometry similar to the synthesis of the Hegelian spirit, and the self-portrait *The Builder*, of 1924, as an early symptom of uncertainty as to the reality of the messianic role of the artist. See Alan C. Birnholz, "El Lissitzky, the Avant-Garde and the Russian Revolution," in *Artforum*, XI, no. 1 (1972), 70–76. On Lissitzky's relationship to Hebraic culture, see Chimen Abramsky, "El Lissitzky as Jewish Illustrator and Typographer," in *Studio International*, CLXXII, no. 822 (1966), 182–185, and A. C. Birnholz, "El Lissitzky and the Jewish Tradition," ibid., CLXXXVI, no. 959 (1976), 130–136. The weight of primitivism and of millenarianism in the formation of the Russian avant-gardes has been emphasized by Markov in his well-known work on Russian futurism (*Russian Futurism: A History* [London: MacGibbon and Kee, 1969]), and has been discussed in (among others) Kenneth Frampton's essay, "Constructivism: The Pursuit of an Elusive Sensibility," in *Oppositions* 6 (1976), 25–43. See also in this regard A. C. Birnholz, "The Russian Avant-Garde and the Russian Tradition," in *Art Journal*, XXXII (winter 1972–1973), 146–149. On the artistic climate of the early 1920s in Russia, see Jean-Paul Bouillon, "Le Retour à l'ordre en Urss 1920–1923," in *Le retour à l'ordre dans les arts plastiques et l'architecture 1919–1925* (Saint-Etienne, 1975), 168–202.

were entirely subordinated to their autonomous collective program and their technological utopia.

After all, already in 1921 Raoul Hausmann, Hans Arp, Puni, and Moholy-Nagy had published in *De Stijl* the manifesto "Aufruf zur Elementaren Kunst."[81] The avant-garde congress held in Düsseldorf from May 29 to May 31, 1922, with the determinative participation of Lissitzky, thus merely picked up again a thread of work begun a good while earlier.

Art as organization of one's entire existence, in the same manner as science and technology: the constructivist resolution of the Düsseldorf congress — signed by van Doesburg, Lissitzky, and Richter, in polemic with many German and French groups[82] — was once again only the founding, on this program, of an international of the avant-garde. The Russian constructivist theory of "art as the construction of life" thus obtained European recognition, and was sanctioned in September 1922, following the dadaist and constructivist congress in Weimar, by the institution of the *Konstruktivistische Internationale schöpferische Arbeitsgemeinschaft* (International Union of Neoplastic Constructivists).[83] Steneberg attributes to Kállai the transformation of the dada meeting in Weimar into a constructivist congress.[84] In reality, it was through van Doesburg himself that the technical-constructive valences of the dada movement had already been singled out as new, positive instruments of communication. It was not only the ideology set forth by the Russian avant-gardes that was now put in parentheses, but the dadaist ideology of protest as well.

---

[81] R. Hausmann, H. Arp, I. Puni, and L. Moholy-Nagy, "Aufruf zur Elementaren Kunst," in *De Stijl,* IV, no. 10 (1921), 156.

[82] See the final manifesto of the Düsseldorf congress, dated 30 May 1922, in *De Stijl,* V, no. 4 (1922). The clash that took place in Düsseldorf between the "unionists" — comprising the Novembergruppe, the Dresden Secession, the Young Rhineland group, the groups l'Albatros and Les Compagnons, and artists such as Däubler, Kokoschka, Rohlfs, Romain Rolland, Kandinsky, Prampolini, Kubicki, etc. — and the constructivist group (Lissitzky, Richter, van Doesburg) is documented in the same number of *De Stijl,* and, in an English translation, in Bann, ed., *The Tradition of Constructivism,* 58–69. See also Joost Baljeu, *Theo van Doesburg* (London, 1974), 49–51 (the chapter "The International Congress of Progressive Artists, Düsseldorf 1922").

[83] T. van Doesburg, H. Richter, K. Maes, Max Burchartz, and Lissitzky, "Konstruktivistische Internationale schöpferische Arbeitsgemeinschaft," in *De Stijl,* V, no. 8 (1922), 113–115. The same number of *De Stijl* contains Prampolini's report on the Weimar congress (199–125) as well as that of the MA group (pp. 125–128). No. 10–11 (1922) of *De Stijl* is dedicated to Lissitzky's *Story of Two Squares.*

[84] Steneberg, *Russische Kunst in Berlin,* 35. Rondolino (*László Moholy-Nagy,* 23–24) points out that the position of the Hungarian constructivists was considerably more politicized than that of Eggeling or Hausmann, citing the text of the MA group presented at the Düsseldorf meeting, in *MA,* VII, no. 8 (1922), 64, and a letter of 1969 from Hausmann to Louise O'Connor.

Participants in the Weimar Congress, 1922: top row, left to right, Max and Lotte Burchartz, Peter Röhl, Vogel, Lucia and Laszlo Moholy-Nagy, Alfred Kemény; middle row, Alexa Röhl, El Lissitzky, Nelly and Theo van Doesburg, Sturtzkopf; bottom row, Werner Graeff, Nini Smit, Harry Scheibe, Cor van Eesteren, Hans Richter, Tristan Tzara, Hans Arp

On this point, van Doesburg, Kállai, and Lissitzky were in perfect accord.

What van Doesburg now proclaimed through his forays into the dadaist sphere (under, as is well known, the pseudonym of I. K. Bonset), and through his dada tour in Holland, undertaken together with Nelly, Huszar, and Schwitters, does not seem, therefore, contradictory.[85] It was not only a programmatic introjection of alienation that led van Doesburg to set himself against the negative avant-gardes, nor was it solely a question of an ultimate attempt at a subjective reunification of the entire arc of the European experiences of rupture. (The latter was the path taken by Hans Richter, perhaps more consistently than by van Doesburg.) The dadaism of the director of *De Stijl* was not that of Ball, nor of Hausmann, much less that of Tzara. Cleansed of any purely iconoclastic matrix, van Doesburg's dadaism reduced the avant-garde to experimentalism; it manifested itself as a list of techniques of communication; it served as the affirmation of a "tradition of the new" and of its "other logic," antithetical to the traditional logic scoffed at by van Doesburg himself in the pages of *Mécano*.[86]

In this sense, the choice of Weimar as the site of the congress was quite significant. Van Doesburg, along with Lissitzky and the European constructivists, viewed the Bauhaus, dominated by Itten's *Vorkurs*, as an anachronistic educational center in which the glorification of anthroposophic-vitalistic myths or of artisan technique presented itself as an alternative to the effort to

[85] The most significant work of van Doesburg the dadaist is the pamphlet *What Is Dada?* (The Hague, 1923). On Dutch dadaism, see K. Schippers (Gerard Stigter), *Holland Dada* (Amsterdam, 1974), in which, in addition to profiling the work of Otto van Rees, A. C. van Rees Dutilh, and Paul Citroen, he dates van Doesburg's earliest interest in dadaism to 1920, citing the article in *Die Nieuwe Amsterdammer* of 8 May 1920, in which van Doesburg wrote, significantly, "Dada wants nothing ... but a nothing in a positive sense." In Baljeu's *Theo van Doesburg*, on the other hand, a letter from van Doesburg to Tzara of 8 December 1918 is cited, in which I. K. Bonset is described as a Dutch dadaist; Baljeu believes that the pseudonym used by van Doesburg to sign his dadaist output was coined between 1916 and 1918, and he posits a direct influence of Hugo Ball (see the chapter "I. K. Bonset: Van Doesburg as a Dadaist and Poet," ibid., 38–39). Van Doesburg's poetry has been published in I. K. Bonset, *Nieuwe Woorbeeldingen. De gedichten van Theo van Doesburg*, with an essay by K. Schippers (Amsterdam, 1975). On van Doesburg and the avant-garde movements involving him, the most authoritative source is the recent volume of van Doesburg's own *Scritti di arte e di architettura*, ed. Sergio Polano (Rome, 1979). On Citroen, see the work by various authors, *Paul Citroen en het Bauhaus* (Utrecht–Antwerp, 1974).

[86] See in particular the "Manifestocontrolarteelaragionpura," in *Mécano*, no. 2 (1922), Italian translation in *Almanacco Dada*, p. 391, as well as the "Cronaca scandalosa dei Paesi Piatti," original in *Der Sturm*, no. 10 (1922), and "Arcachitettonica" (an attack against Berlage's museum in the Hague), in *Mécano*, no. 1 (1922), Italian translation in *Almanacco Dada*, 390–391.

unify the techniques of mass communication. The congress of 1922 was thus an obvious provocation (parallel to the noted clashes between van Doesburg and the Bauhaus), which was immediately received and absorbed by Gropius. The *Bauhauswoche* of 1923, with the exhibition and the manifestations that marked the official moment of the "rationalist" turning point of the school, took place, and probably not by chance, at the same time as the great exhibition of student work of the Metfak in Moscow.

Both the Bauhaus and de Stijl had as their primary objective — from different points of view — the synthesis of avant-garde experiments; a number of the points that emerged in the 1922 congress would be taken up again the following year by the Bauhaus. The manifesto signed by the Central Committee of the International Union of Neoplastic Constructivists insisted, in fact, upon collective work, on an international, antisentimental art, on an *art as organization*, as reformer of social life. "This international," wrote van Doesburg, Richter, the Belgian Karel Maes, Max Burchartz, and Lissitzky,[87] "is not the result of some humanitarian, idealistic, or political sentiment, but springs *from the same amoral and elementary principles* on which both science and technology are based."

The avant-garde, brought back to its elementary principles, was thus obliged to reveal its cards completely, to recognize its own origins in "negative thought," to declare once again not only its own non-political nature, but also its own *immoralism*.

At this point, one might continue to follow the complex affair of the exchanges between Soviet avant-gardes and European avant-gardes, from the great Lissitzky exhibition of 1923 in Berlin, to the relations with the Kestner Society of Hanover and with Alexander Dorner, to the growth of the elementarist reviews — *G*, *Merz*, and the Swiss *ABC*.[88] But the affair would by this time be a different one.

Between 1922 and 1923, in fact, this historical paradox

[87] Van Doesburg, "Konstruktivistische." My italics.

[88] On the fortunes of the review *ABC* (1924 – 1928), see Jacques Gubler, *Nationalisme et internationalisme dans l'architecture moderne de la Suisse* (Lausanne: L'age d'homme, 1975), 109 ff. Of great interest is the story of Polish constructivism, particularly for the work of artists such as Henryk Berlewi and Mieczyslaw Szczuka, who were linked to German circles in the early 1920s, or of Wladislaw Strzeminski and Katarzyna Kobro, who were close to Malevich and to the Soviet postrevolutionary debate. See the documentation in the volume edited by Ryszard Stanislawski, *Constructivism in Poland, 1922 – 1936*, catalogue of the exhibition at the Folkwang Museum, Essen, and at the Rijksmuseum Kröller-Müller, Otterlo, 1973, partially reprinted with additional material in the catalogue *L'avanguardia polacca* (Milan, 1979).

Kurt Schwitters, Mz 273. Halberstadt, *collage, 1921*

became apparent: the Soviet avant-garde, introduced as a paradigm of the art of a developing socialism into a Germany permeated with expressionist pathos, found itself objectively carrying out the task of revealing that the only "politicalness" possible for the avant-garde was that of announcing the advent of a universe of *non-values, amoral, elementary*: exactly the technological universe of the organized development of great capital denounced by Grosz as a terrifying universe "without quality."

The ideology of production or, better, *the image of the ideology of highly mechanized work* became, from here on, the authentic manifesto of the *Constructivist International*, above and beyond the chance divergencies separating the experiences of the different groups. All of the history that follows is affected by the failures and frustrations suffered by the avant-gardes in their attempt to "realize the ideology," in the capitalist West just as in Soviet Russia.

Yet the two congresses, at Weimar and Düsseldorf, especially because of the polemical tone that characterized them, did not lead to new institutional organizations of intellectual work. The apparatus set up by German Social Democracy was by now in an evident state of crisis and, if need be, replaceable by new "technical" supports of management. The most constructive demands expressed in 1922 would, significantly, find an outlet in the founding of CIAM.

The ideological unification was, in reality, already in the cards: in the discovery of the silence surrounding the *sign*, that residue, that insuppressible boundary that remained after the dadaist devastation. The negative, having arrived at the limit that separates language from silence, was in a position to organize syntactical structures deprived of referents — or, better, full of referents intent on verifying themselves.

But at this point the ambiguous oscillation of the *Proun* between the real and the unreal became anachronistic. The "wicked transgression" composed itself into a series of codes. The avant-garde, more or less consciously, consigned to architecture and to the techniques of the visual tranformation of the environment the task of testing in a concrete fashion its own productivity.[89]

---

[89] In this regard, I consider highly important Ludwig Hilberseimer's article, "Anmerkungen zur neuen Kunst" (1923), reprinted in the pamphlet *Zehn Jahre Novembergruppe*, 52 – 57, which I reproduce in its entirety: "Now we need barbarians. Now it is necessary to have lived very close to God, not to have studied him through books. One must be able to look at natural life in a magical way; one must have strength and even rage. The time of delicacy and of pleasure is past. The time of passion begins.' With these words Charles-Louis Philippe character-

izes clearly the spiritual aspect of early expressionism. The barbaric was a means of rejuvenation for art. Or, as Gauguin once said of himself: we went way, way back, even farther back than the horses of the Parthenon, we went back as far as the wooden horses of our childhood. Parallel to expressionism and stimulated by it, the science of art has advanced to the farthest point. To the most primitive, to the most original. To grasp prehistoric art and exotic art and their parallel phenomena contemporaneously, the creative productions of children and of the insane. The most extraordinary and most bizarrely grotesque forms in prehistory and in the world of the exotic are the manifestations of the magical. Manifestations of the metaphysical. In children and in the insane, interpretations of spiritual landscapes of the world. Of the unshakable belief in one's own face. Primitive and infantile artistic elements have steadily determined the formal world of expressionism. Even if with the elementary expressionists we can by no means speak of imitation, they are nonetheless strongly influenced by those suggestive elementary forms.

But for the expressionists, an element much more determining than form is color. It is their domain. Following in the tradition of medieval painting with its strong colors, the expressionists use color as an element of psychological effect. The Russians in particular carried it to its extreme consequences. Using the psychological element of color, expressionism has created a transformed world, a world almost completely new. For it, color is music. It is a source of infinite possibilities of variation. It uncovers the most profound secrets. It illuminates the optical image of the world.

Cubism is essentially a structure of planes mediating contrasting subdivisions. It has recognized the particular ordinance of the work of art, like an extraordinary organism with iron-clad laws of structure. It has consciously touched on the elements of all formations, returning to geometric-cubic form. It has recognized the identity between matter and form. In cubist works, in fact, one sees the contrasts of manufacture and varied materials forced into unity by compositional points of view. An artistic principle, which the *Merzkunst* has systematically elaborated.

Notwithstanding its inclination to objectivity, cubism ended up, like expressionism, in subjective speculations. The problem of anthropomorphic figuration continued to occupy too much of its time.

In addition to color, the means to the realization of any artistic interest is form. It dominates chaos. It creates organisms. If the process of forming is also transformed into a game, into mere determination of static functions and of beautiful relationships, a certain uprooting takes place. A rigidifying of the formal structure. The disappearance of intensity. A certain self-suppression. A reaction takes place. A conscious inclination toward the past. Thus primitivism, exoticism, and infantilism arose within expressionism. In response to a rigidified cubism, a turning to classicism. All these intentions that link themselves to the past are but attempts to substitute an intellectual rapport with the past for the lost tradition. But it is far from a return to nature. Expressed in all these aspirations is the search for the law that the art of the past manifests in almost all of its works. But every link to the past is destined to lead to eclecticism. The true work of art will always be born only from the chaos of time. Only in this way can its image take on sense.

Dadaism brought with it a general activity that had a vivifying effect on art. Its effect in Germany has been essentially political. In Switzerland and France it led to the continuation of cubism, to a purely abstract art. A phenomenon parallel to Russian suprematism.

Suprematism carried non-objective to its ultimate possibilities. The fact that a suprematist could cover a square uniformly with paint applied flatly meant the end of abstractionism. The complete nullification of materiality. But at the same time, also the maximum concentration. The will straining to the maximum, toward final unity. Suprematism breaks up the stereometric figurative elements of cubism into planimetric elements. Thus it creates a resulting painting of surfaces. The suprematists seek the point of nothingness in art. They close the process of analytical reduction. They are waiting for synthetic forms still to come.

With great resolve, the constructivists have traveled a new path. That of reality. In their first constructions, which were not yet utilitarian, one can recognize a very clear will to take possession of the real. From construction in painting the constructivists have moved on to the construction of objects. To architecture in the broadest sense of the word. Constructivism is the logical consequence of methods of work that are based on the collectivity of our time. Thus it has a base that is of a general rather than a subjective nature. It perceives the subordination of art to society without reserve, as of all of life. It seeks its elements in the expressions of our mechanized and industrialized time. Mathematical clarity, geometrical rigor, functional organization, extreme economy, and the most exact possible constructiveness are problems that are not only technical but also eminently artistic. They determine what is properly essential in our epoch. The constructivist method brings any object into the ambit of formation. Not suppressing liveliness, but forming a reality.

The works of the constructivists are, when all is said and done, nothing but experiments with materials. They consciously work toward a solution to the new problems posed by material and by form. Theirs are merely works of a transition toward functional architectural constructions. The ultimate goal is a well-disciplined preparation for architecture."

Translated by Pellegrino d'Acierno and Robert Connolly

El Lissitzky, Proun 6B, *1921*

Postscript: Critical History
and the Labors of Sisyphus

Joan Ockman

> Sisyphus, proletarian of the gods, powerless and
> rebellious, knows the whole extent of his
> wretched condition: it is what he thinks of during
> his descent. The lucidity that was to constitute
> his torture at the same time crowns his victory.
> There is no fate that cannot be surmounted by
> scorn.
>
> Albert Camus, *The Myth of Sisyphus*

Tafuri's critical subject is architecture, ideologies, utopia, historical space, language, techniques, institutions, urban administration. In the preceding essay, excerpted from his recent book, *La sfera e il labirinto* (1980), he views through several facets of this multiple lens the role and function of the architect in a society whose vision of itself is increasingly collective and technological. The focus is on a crucial moment in the vicissitudes of high modernist ideology: the encounter between the avant-gardes in the Soviet Union and in Germany around 1922. Berlin is seen as the historical meeting ground between East and West. Tafuri traces the transformation of expressionist and populist tendencies in German culture after the war, through the newly politicized energies of the Berlin dada, into the internationalized movement of constructivism proclaimed in the congresses of Weimar and Düsseldorf and in the polemical manifestos signed by Lissitzky, van Doesburg, Moholy-Nagy, Arp, and others. In this complex and "negative" trajectory, the Western European avant-garde ends up, paradoxically, as the anticipatory protagonist of an "objective" aesthetic that mirrors the technological-rational ideology of capitalist production.

The only example of the critical historian's praxis in this magazine, the chapter represents a classic application of Tafuri's methodology. He lays this out in his introduction to *La sfera e il labirinto*, titled "The Historical 'Project.'"[1] Here Tafuri defines the historian's — his own — task as follows: "To construct a history which, after having shattered and upset the apparent compactness of the real, after having shifted the ideological barriers which hide the complexity of the strategies of domination, arrives at the heart of those strategies: arrives, that is, at their modes of production." (It should be noted that Demetri Porphyrios's paper in this publication — especially the last part — is largely a reformulation and defense of the Tafurian position.) Tafuri's military rhetoric, which aggressively views all institutions, architecture among them, as "strategies of domination" linked to the advancement of capitalism, and which sees the enemy as ideology — not because it is evil or erroneous in any moral sense but because it dissimulates "the real" — then pulls back to question its own objectives and efficacy. At this point the imagery shifts from that of Marx to that of Nietzsche and Foucault. The critical historian must rid himself of a tragic nostalgia for fullness, for closure; he must harbor no illusions about his own powers to demystify historical relations once and for all simply by forcing them "into crisis." The writing of history is not hermeneutics, however complexly it goes about comprehending its subject, and its goal is not to reveal truth, but to go beyond itself. "What," Tafuri asks, "will allow me to pass from a history written in the plural to a questioning of that same plurality?" The answer he gives himself is realism, patience, constant vigilance. The analogy is to personal history, to psychoanalysis: "Once a system of power is isolated, its genealogy cannot be offered as a subject complete in itself: the analysis must go further; it must make previously isolated fragments collide with each other; it must question the limits which it has set up. Regarded as 'labor,' in fact, analysis has no end; it is, as Freud recognizes, by its very nature *infinite.*"

The labor of writing history, then, is provisional and interminable — and in this sense would seem to have as much affinity with the iterative activity of Sisyphus as with the cyclical forces of the marketplace. For while every deconstruction should lead back to a "re-montage" in order to avoid freezing fragments into autonomous signs (here Tafuri makes his critique of the methods of Foucault and Derrida), the historian must guard against the complacency of allowing his reconstituted language to become institutional in itself, a monumental "imaginary library,"

---

[1] A version of this introduction appears in *Oppositions* 17 (summer 1979). Quotations in the present article are from a manuscript translation by Pellegrino d'Acierno and Robert Connolly.

and ultimately another project of domination. This attitude, pushed to its logical conclusion, would at first seem to provide the objection to a kind of dialectical incrementalism in the realm of historical knowledge such as Fredric Jameson has proposed in the name of a "Gramscian alternative" in the realm of architecture; that is, to any kind of gradual forwarding mechanism in the consciousness of history. Since history is written under the sign of capitalism, it is always at risk of co-optation within the intellectual marketplace; thus it must constantly resort to the violence of exploding its own conclusions. Tafuri, however, does not go this far. Conscious of the dangers involved, he nevertheless admits a limited notion of "progress" into the endless historiographic cycle of deconstruction and reconstruction; I shall return to this aspect of his argument shortly.

But the practice of architectural history is also "difficult" in a more specific way, in terms of its subject matter. Because the subject is exceptionally complex and plural, in Tafuri's view, it is especially recalcitrant to dialectical resolution. The architectural work, the construction of a physical space, represents a battleground of a multitude of colliding forces, a highly volatile synthesis of developments in the modes and relations of production and consumption, on the one hand, and intellectual or abstract labor, on the other. This makes the architectural historian's task a particularly delicate one. Resisting the distortive tendencies to simplification lurking in operative criticism, architectural history must be able to describe both the concrete and abstract aspects of architecture critically and exhaustively, and to insert itself into the dialectical gap between these competing base and superstructural forces. This gap is the historical space in which ideology flourishes, and it is the passage of ideology — or rather, a whole spectrum of ideologies: institutional, progressive (utopian), regressive, reformist — from the superstructure into the domain of the real that opens up a field of urgent historical work, one that leads to further projects: "It is useless to cry over a proven fact: ideology has changed into reality, even if the romantic dream of the intellectuals who proposed to guide the destiny of the productive universe has remained, logically, in the superstructural sphere of utopia. As historians, our task is to reconstruct lucidly the road traversed by intellectual labor, recognizing the contingent tasks to which a new organization of labor can respond."

Having set himself this task, Tafuri rejects the ahistorical perspective of structuralism and the disciplinary hermetics of the *nouvelle critique* as an exclusive method. Against the *mise en abîme* of the "magic circle of language" and the pleasurable fascinations of multiplying "weightless metaphors" within a Barthesian "system of ambiguity" of pure textuality, Tafuri requires the critical historian to balance his labors on the precarious boundary between *analysis* and *project*, between detachment and participation (without, however, overstepping the bounds of participation into operative criticism); in the language of the Russian formalist critics, "to measure the real incidence of language on the extra-linguistic series to which it is connected." This does not preclude investigations within the realm of architectural language itself:

> To insert the history of architecture into the range of a history of the social division of labor by no means means regressing to a "vulgar Marxism"; it does not at all mean erasing the specific characteristics of architecture itself. On the contrary, they will be emphasized by means of a reading capable of placing — on the basis of verifiable parameters — the real meaning of the choices of projects into the dynamics of the productive transformations that they set into motion, that they slow up, that they try to impede.

Moreover, different levels of analysis may be appropriate to the wide variation in architectural subjects: a Roman triumphal arch and a project for urban renewal, for example. In attributing a broad and flexible meaning to the concept of architecture, Tafuri thus defends himself against accusations of methodological eclecticism on the basis of the "multiform and disorganized" nature of architecture as a discipline.

Provisory as it may be, the "reading based on verifiable parameters" can lead to real knowledge. By knowledge, Tafuri does not have in mind any "universal truth," any *wirkliche Historie*; his "genealogical" as opposed to teleological view "does not counterpose itself against history as does the lofty and profound view of the philosopher to the mole-like gaze of the scholar; on the contrary, it opposes the metahistorical unfolding of ideal meanings and indefinite teleologies" (Tafuri is here quoting from Foucault). Thus, knowledge is "made up of little, not obvious, truths, arrived at by a rigorous method" (here quoting Foucault, who is quoting the Nietzsche of *Human, All Too Human*). In this, Tafuri echoes the Rossi of the first lines of a *A Scientific Autobiography* ("To what, then, could I have aspired in my craft? Certainly to small things, having seen that the possibility of great ones was historically precluded"); indeed, it is an attitude that has affinities with much late modern or postmodern thought, and evidently is symptomatic of our time.

Still, it is this very reservation of the possibility of accumulating small truths that pulls the Tafurian project back from the brink of pure nihilism to something a little like the incrementalist notion mentioned earlier. The model is psychoanalysis; the metaphor seems to be mining: "[Historical] work, then, must proceed gradually, constructing its own methods as supports in perennial tranformation ... temporary barriers ... 'shift the stones' by removing its own stones." And even at these reduced margins of efficacy, we realize that the historian is granted, relatively speaking, a privileged position. His labors, interminable and compulsory as they may be, vouchsafe the rewards of an increasing consciousness through what Nietzsche considered to be the supreme and only freedom, "the acceptance of the necessary."

In this context, however, one cannot help but observe that the radical scaling down of the historian's ambitions closely parallels the fate of the aspirations of the architectural avant-garde in Tafuri's version. In other words, there is a convergence, not only between the story Tafuri narrates — one notes how often he treats his history as a "story," an "adventure," as if its subject were fictional — and his point of view (world view), but also between the story and the method of narration. It is this that gives the Tafurian version of history its suffocating atmosphere of closure, despite the Nietzschean liberation it claims to effect. The critique of ideology becomes bound up with the failure of utopian ideology (i.e., the collapse of utopian thought into ideology), and the historian's task is confined not simply to describing this failure of avant-garde aspirations, but to responding to it, and reproducing it, methodologically. Critical distance — that very "distance which separates words from things" — in this way gets breached by an "inclination toward the other," a profound intellectual sympathy in the writing about favorite subjects. So when Tafuri writes in chapter four, "Schwitters thus denies resolutely the utopia of a 'political' art in favor of a production of formal objects conceived as a pure clash of neutral signs," it is difficult not to read into this Tafuri's identification of his own situation as historian with that of Schwitters as artist; Schwitters emerges in these pages as both herald and personal hero. The Schwitters model mirrors Tafuri's own preference for a purely formal architecture — for example, his interest in such architects as the New York Five — over an engaged but compromised one: "To the deceptive attempts to give architecture an ideological dress, I shall always prefer the sincerity of those who have the courage to speak of that silent and outdated 'purity'; even if this, too, still harbors an ideological inspiration, pathetic in its anachronism" (*Architecture and Utopia*, p. ix).

This leads one to question to what degree Tafuri's method has been determined by his content and, more problematically, vice-versa. Fredric Jameson makes a similar point, considering the problem endemic to the "genre" of "dialectical historiography" in general: "The principal 'event' of such dialectical histories — the contradiction itself, the fatal reversal of this or that aesthetic solution as it comes to grief against its own material underside — necessarily determines the form of their narrative closure and the kind of 'ending' they are led to project.... Tafuri's 'pessimism' is thus to be seen as a formal necessity of the generic structure of his text." Such a generic determination of the "story line" is, one would think, structurally closer to the domain of the fiction writer — the artist generally — than to that of the historian who affirms the necessity of detachment. The historian's relation to his subject becomes a *mimetic* one. And in the sense that through the redundancy of subject matter and theory the one inevitably acts as an instrument of verification for the other, the criticism seems very much to be an operative one, an ideology, notwithstanding the fact that it operates *negatively*. Like the Old Testament prophet it tells architecture what it *should not be*, even if the prescription is, by virtue of its negativity, unprogrammatic.

This brings us squarely to the issue of where the critical historian stands with respect to his subject. Can critical history, as Porphyrios would suggest, "conduct its analysis from outside the discursive site defined by its subject matter"? By virtue of an Althusserian notion of the "semi-autonomy" of levels of social practice, is it credible that the historian can, to use Porphyrios's language again, "lie outside the notions, representations, images, modes of action, gestures, attitudes, and practical norms that govern the architecture he studies"? Tomas Llorens, in an article entitled "Manfredo Tafuri: Neo-Avant-Garde and History" (*Architectural Design* 51, no. 6/7, 1981), suggests that Tafuri "pushes his search for the mechanisms of ideological determinism well beyond the limits of epistemological plausibility," since as historian he has no possibility ever to stand outside the *global* ideological system that he himself has postulated. Trapped within a closed universe in which fields have fluid boundaries and all social practices are contaminated by ideology, Tafuri's approach, in Llorens's view, "is characterized by a moral mistrust of any intention toward effective social transformation, and by an emphasis on the rule-governed status of cultural phenomena.... The attempt to narrate such a world results necessarily in a discourse where all shapes and figures are erased by the monotonous repetition of the same judgment; a judgment which

187

always uses the same concept as a predicate, namely that everything amounts to "silence. " To some extent, of course, Llorens's viewpoint is echoed by the critique of dialectical historiography made by Jameson.

If so, then starting from Tafuri's point of view, can the historian have any ultimate effectiveness beyond small increases in his own consciousness of his burden? Inside history, interminably pushing fragments of provisory knowledge uphill in order to prepare them to roll back down again, is he capable of envisioning, and allowing, any future that is different from the present? Tafuri, in fact, struggles much harder with this question — even at the risk of epistemological contradiction — than Llorens's negative judgment indicates; in this sense, Jameson provides a much more sympathetic and nuanced reading. One must also keep in mind that the rhetoric shifts somewhat from *Theories and History of Architecture* (first published in 1968) to *Architecture and Utopia* (1973), to the more recent volume, which is also the most reticent in terms of a direct political polemic. In the latter writing, as we have seen, the historian is portrayed as constantly involved in a struggle against limits: of his own discipline, of his own ideological entanglement in history, of the global social and economic system. It is the rhetorical tension between resigned intellectual acceptance and a more activist struggle against an enemy defined as ideology that makes Tafuri's history politically engaged, even if it would be "crass idealism" — another utopian project — for us to interpret him as suggesting that the identification of intolerable realities through historical analysis "is sufficient to bring about their effective and actual elimination." No doubt this is a painful position to maintain, and it generates Tafuri's relentless and obsessive self-interrogation into his role as historian; one thinks of the "unreasonable" affirmation of Samuel Beckett's narrator in *The Unnamable*: "In the silence you don't know, you must go on, I can't go on, I'll go on."

Nevertheless, leaving aside for the moment the problem of the autonomy of two "adjectivally" related disciplines such as architectural history and architectural practice, we find Tafuri, at least in his earlier two books, insisting on a differentiation on the basis of *function* between the disciplines of architecture and politics. Doing so allows him to assert that the domain of revolutionary transformation is neither architecture nor architectural history; rather, the effectiveness of ideological criticism is to push thought and action away from any false "hopes in design" into the only possible realm of action, politics proper:

It is useless to propose purely architectural

188

alternatives. The search for an alternative within the structures that condition the very character of architectural design is indeed an obvious contradiction in terms. Reflection on architecture, inasmuch as it is a criticism of the concrete "realized" ideology of architecture itself, cannot but go beyond this and arrive at a specifically political dimension. (*Architecture and Utopia*, p. 182)

Likewise, in *Theories and History* Tafuri speaks of the historian's work as "political activity — even if indirectly political" (p. 236). Finally, in a subtle but perhaps significant shift, in his introduction to *La sfera e il labirinto* he admits a "delicately political problem": "One fights a social production with alternative social productions; this seems to us indisputable"; and operative criticism, after all that has been said against it, and however one has tried to remain innocent of it, is "a road which nonetheless one cannot avoid following."

All of this does not make Tafuri's view of architectural *practice* much less negative (although, as Jameson points out, in writing about actual projects he at times seems more sanguine). Tafuri's view seems to be that the practice of architecture within the present economy is politically useless (even if culturally inevitable — and possibly even sublimely useless) except insofar as it provides the fodder for the critical historian to galvanize (indirectly) a revolution in the political domain. But how much power, in Tafuri's mind, does the historian really have? Aside from the underlying egocentricity of assigning the historian a privileged status as potential fulcrum of social transformation, Tafuri seems to harbor a confidence in the ultimate possibilities of global political action that, in the absence of historical evidence, does not seem more warranted today than a confidence in architectural action.

I realize that this last subject is, strictly speaking, outside of Tafuri's thematics as architectural historian. Still, his argument appears to depend upon it if the *gioco di pazienza* is not to be taken solely as an attempt to realize the contradictions of a "liberating" — but austere — nihilism through the endgame of architectural history. What is needed is further articulation, in the anatomical as much as the linguistic sense, of the precise relations, the ideological junctures, between architectural practice, architectural history, and political action.

Selected Bibliography

The following list includes the readings of the study group as well as some material related to the articles in this publication.

Althusser, Louis. *For Marx*. Translated by Ben Brewster. New York: Vintage Books, 1969.

Benjamin, Walter. "Allegory and Trauerspiel." In *The Origin of German Tragic Drama*. Translated by John Osborne. London: New Left Books, 1977, 157 – 235.

"The Author as Producer." In *Reflections*. Translated by Edmund Jephcott. New York: Harcourt Brace Jovanovich, 1978.

"The Work of Art in the Age of Mechanical Reproduction." In *Illuminations*. Translated by Harry Zohn. New York: Schocken Books, 1969, 217 – 251.

Colquhoun, Alan. *Essays in Architectural Criticism: Modern Architecture and Historical Change*. Cambridge, Mass: MIT Press, 1981.

Della Volpe, Galvano. *Critique of Taste*. Translated by Michael Caesar. Oxford: New Left Books, 1978.

Frampton, Kenneth. "Towards a Critical Regionalism: Six Points for an Architecture of Resistance." In *The Anti-Aesthetic: Essays on Postmodern Culture*. Edited by Hal Foster. Port Townsend, Washington: Bay Press, 1983, 16 – 30.

Gramsci, Antonio. *Selections from the Prison Notebooks of Antonio Gramsci*. Edited and translated by Quintin Hoare and Geoffrey Nowell Smith. New York: International Publishers, 1971.

Habermas, Jürgen. "Modernity versus Postmodernity." Translated by Seyla Ben-Habib. *New German Critique*, no. 22 (winter 1981), 3 – 14. Reprinted as "Modernity — An Incomplete Project" in *The Anti-Aesthetic*, 3 – 15.

Horkheimer, Max, and Adorno, Theodor W. *Dialectic of Enlightenment*. Translated by John Cumming. New York: Continuum, 1982.

Jameson, Fredric. *Marxism and Form: Twentieth-Century Dialectical Theories of Literature*. Princeton: Princeton Univ. Press, 1971.

   The Political Unconscious: Narrative as a Socially Symbolic Act. Ithaca, N.Y.: Cornell Univ. Press, 1981, esp. 206 – 297.

Lefèbvre, Henri. *Everyday Life and the Modern World*. Translated by Sacha Rabinovitch. London: Penguin Press, 1971.

Llorens, Tomas. "Manfredo Tafuri: Neo-Avant-Garde and History," *On the Methodology of Architectural History*. *Architectural Design* 51, no. 6/7 (1981), 83 – 95.

Tafuri, Manfredo. *Architecture and Utopia: Design and Capitalist Development*. Translated by Barbara Luigia La Penta. Cambridge, Mass.: MIT Press, 1980.

   "The Historical Project." Translated by Stephen Sartarelli and Diane Ghirardo. *Oppositions* 17 (summer 1979), 55 – 75.

   Theories and History of Architecture. Translated by Giorgio Verrecchia. New York: Harper and Row, 1976.

Williams, Raymond. *Marxism and Literature*. Oxford: Oxford Univ. Press, 1977.

This book is Smyth-sewn and printed on acid-free paper.
The typeface is Palatino.